CW00434772

THE TURBULENT TOUR

The Turbulent Tour – The Story of the 1954 Rugby league Tour

© Tom Mather

The moral right of Tom Mather as the author has been identified.

Any photographs in the book are from private collections or Trove Newspaper archives unless otherwise credited. No copyright has been intentionally breached, please contact the author if you believe there has been a breach of copyright.

This book is copyright under the Berne Convention. All rights are reserved. It is sold subject to the condition that it shall not by way of trade or otherwise, be lent, resold, hired out or otherwise circulated without the publisher's prior consent in any form of binding or cover other than that in which it is published and without a similar condition being imposed on the subsequent purchaser. The book shall not be electronically transmitted to another person or persons.

Tom Mather

July 2018

ACKNOWLEDGEMENTS

There are many reasons just why a book gets written, it could simply be the writer is interested enough in a topic to sit at a computer and write. On the other hand, it could be a chance comment or remark that attracts the writers interest. Having written a series of books covering the tours down under by the Rugby League between the two World Wars, I felt that was enough. Then a comment on Facebook by Karl Silcock the son of Nat Silcock and Grandson of Nat senior both tourists sparked my interest. He said someone should write about the 1954 tour as there was a lot going on during that tour.

I began to do a little research and the end result is this book. There are other people to thank for their help none more so than Emma Burgham the Archive Assistant at Huddersfield University. It was she who unearthed the various reports produced following this turbulent and tempestuous visit to the Antipodes. Terry Williams at The NRL Museum was as ever a font of information which he willingly shared with me. He also very kindly provided a number of illustrations reproduced in the book. The reporters who covered events on and off the field all those years ago also deserve thanks, they covered some torrid events on that tour with clarity and honesty. I hope that comes through in the book. To all those players who participated in the tour both Australian and New Zealanders along with the tourists go my thanks for without them there would be no book.

Finally, to my wife Janet for once more proof reading, correcting and suggesting additions to the manuscript my heartfelt thanks.

INTRODUCTION

The tenth tour by the Rugby League to Australia and New Zealand gained fame for all the wrong reasons. Right from the outset there was controversy firstly for the decision to send the players down under by air travel immediately the season ended, rather than by sea. Many in the game thought the decision innovative while others thought it fraught with danger. Certainly, the clubs were happy as they retained the services of their players right up to the end of the season. Equally important was the fact the players would be home much earlier and so be available as the new season was beginning.

No one gave any consideration to the fact the players would be coming to the end of a long hard season and then just a week or so later be playing in the middle of the Australian season. Secondly there was also no thought given to the underlying ill feelings that existed between the players from the two countries particularly the Australians. They had failed to retain the Ashes on the 1952-53 tour and there was a deepseated perception that one English player in particular was guilty of underhand if not illegal tactics.

Those ill feelings would come to the surface very quickly in the tour. In truth they were stoked up by the newspapers even before the tourists arrived in Sydney.

The English players were equally guilty of seeking retribution for perceived injustices from the Australian and New Zealand referees but had one great disadvantage over their opponents. Given the flight to Australia took only four days and two days later the first match of the tour was played there was no time for the players to 'gel' as a team, no time to really get to know each other. It led to a situation where the players and the managers never really knew just which thirteen players were the best to play in the Test matches. Equally it meant players were not playing games consistently with set team mates.

It was a tour which saw:-

The players travel by air throughout the tour.
Trouble flair up in and after the game at Mackay.
The so called 'Battle of Rockhampton'.
Trouble in the second Test in Brisbane.
A match abandoned by the referee for foul play.
Accusations of rough play in Auckland in two games.
The final game of the tour dubbed the dirtiest of the tour.
One player constantly hounded by the press during the tour and walk off the field in the final game.
Constant claims of dirty play against the tourists.
One of the managers taken to court in Sydney.
The claim that an international 'black list' had been established following the tour.

A number of players emerge from the tour that would become 'greats of the game'.
Reports on the foul play on tour from the three countries being written and changes made to the game as a result.

It was all of these factors and many more that lead to the tour being the most troubled and turbulent in the history of the game. It would cause the Australian and New Zealand authorities to formally write to the council complaining of the behaviour of some players and the illegal tactics employed by members of the tour party. The English authorities for their part were forced to defend the two managers and make recommendations designed to prevent future incidents on tours. There was also a suggestion that a blacklist of troublesome players was drawn up by the Rugby League authorities following the tour.

CHAPTER ONE

The 1954 tour to Australia was one which was eagerly anticipated by all, perhaps not for all the right reasons. The tour to England by the Australians back in 1952 had seen the home side regain the Ashes following a two to one win in the Test series. The Aussies when they left for England had been referred to by the rugby league press in Sydney as perhaps the worst ever to leave Australian shores. They were considered by many to be the weakest tour party the country had ever sent on tour.

That said Clive Churchill and his men managed to win twenty-three games, draw one and lose only three, not a bad record by any standard. The problem for the tourists was that two of those losses occurred in the first and second Test matches and so they gave up the Ashes won in 1950 on home soil. The opinion of most people in the game was that for the first two Tests the Australian team simple did not turn up. Certainly, they did not play with the fluency and verve they had displayed in other games on the tour.

It would be true to say that feelings between the two countries were not at their best for having seen England win the first Test 19-6 and the second by 21-5 all expected the home country to secure a whitewash in the series. The tourists on the other hand had other ideas and intended to win by hook or by boot. The third and final

Test was to be played at Odsal Stadium the home of Bradford Northern and over 30,500 spectators turned out to witness the event. It turned out not to be a game for the purist, but rather a game for the pugilist. It was an ugly bad tempered and violent affair reminiscent of the Test played in Brisbane back 1932 the so-called Battle of Brisbane Test. Fighting broke out in all parts of the ground, punches were thrown with great regularity as was the boot. It prompted the newspapers to describe the game in such terms as disgraceful, shameful and disgusting. It certainly was not a good advert for the game but the Aussies took the prize winning 27-7 thus avoiding a white wash in the series.

Following the match, the England vice-captain Ernest Ward was so disgusted he refused to shake hands with the Australians walking straight off the field and into the dressing room. There is a quote from the England loose forward Ken Traill in an article in the Sydney Morning Herald on the Monday following the game. Traill said:-

"None could say our forwards or the Aussie pack were footballers today. We acted like12 animals- like 12 busy bears fighting over a bun.

I have never played in a rougher match and was surprised at referee Dobson letting it get that way."

The game left a nasty taste in the mouth for both sides each blaming the other for the dreadful scenes. It also saw both sides store up memories in order that scores real or imaginary could be settled two years down the track when the English visited the Antipodes. It that were not enough there was another nemesis that prayed on the minds of the Australians. This time it was not a particular team but rather a particular player and not a particularly big player at that. The player in question was the St. Helens centre Duggie Greenall.

Greenall it seems had caused all sorts of consternation in the Aussie camp whenever he had faced them. Such was the ferocity and manner in which he tackled opposing players and the effect his tackles had on them that it raised questions for the visitors. The tourists accused Greenall of actually playing with plaster of Paris strapped to his forearm. It was of course nonsense as the referee checked players before they went onto the field. The problem was that Greenall had perfected the timing and delivery of the perfect stiff-arm tackle. Back in his day such actions were not seen in the same light as they are today!

When the Aussies had played at Knowsley Road against St. Helens it seems, if reports are to be believed that each and every Aussie player at one time or another were on the receiving end of a Greenall tackle. During the game it became apparent that Greenall had his forearm strapped for some reason or another and perhaps this gave rise to the stories taken back to Australia.

Following that game an Aussie player when interviewed by the press claimed that all the Aussies heard when they took to the field and during game was the crowd roaring 'Give 'em Mammy Duggie'. The player went on to say we did not know what that meant but we very soon found out.

It seems that the tourists were to be on the receiving end of Mammy on a number of other occasions for Greenall was to oppose then in both the second and third Test matches. In the second Test Greenall had cleaned out the Aussie centre Hazzard with one of his special tackles. Hazzard was carried unconscious from the field that afternoon. To rub salt in the wounds he also turned out for Lancashire against them. It must be pointed out that Greenall was famous for his rendition of the Al Jolson song Mammy and perhaps the crowd were making reference to the song rather than Greenall's ferocious tackling. Whichever it was the Australians went home with stories of the Saints centre which as all such stories always seem to grow in more and more lurid detail as time passed. There is no doubt many players down under were waiting to both see this monster and also take revenge for the perceived injustices he was able to get away with in the old country.

While all the past troubles of that 1952 tour were gently bubbling away on the back boiler the Council of the Rugby League were creating problems of their own.

They had made the decision that the selection for the tour would be in the hands of a committee made up of twelve members. All seemed to have forgotten or perhaps ignored the old maxim that **A camel is a horse designed by a committee.** It was a decision that they were to rue a little way down the track.

The other decision that was made was in truth, while ground breaking, was to have a detrimental effect on both the players selected and the very tour itself. They made the decision to send the players to Australia not via the seas in favour of the air. They forgot or chose to forget that the six-week seas voyage enabled players to rest and recuperate from a hard season. Now the players would literally end their English season one week and be playing on Australian soil a week or so later. The other factor which was ignored or perhaps not recognised back then was the debilitating effects of long flights and jet lag.

It was after all these issues had been discussed by the Council that plans were formulated to get the tour, the third since the end of the war organised. Given the experience of organising such tours that the Council had available the tour process began.

CHAPTER TWO

When the Rugby League Council meet to begin the arrangements for the 1954 tour they were very well aware of what was required from a practical point of view. They were after all organising the tenth such tour to Australia and New Zealand. They simply went into 'tour mode' appointed a sub-committee and got on with the business of ordering playing equipment and the likes. The only innovation to cause concern was the decision made to fly out to Australia. The practicalities were simple, flights were booked on a Quantas Constellation aircraft that was to fly from London. That said at £460 per person return, it represented an initial outlay of around £13,000 for council and then there was the internal flights to take into consideration.

The journey would see the players fly from London to Rome on the first leg of the journey. From there the flight would take them to Karachi, then onto Singapore before landing in Darwin in the far north of Australia. From there the last leg would see them fly into Sydney. The whole trip was expected to take just under four days which many saw as a great advantage. The question was, advantage to who, the players or the clubs. The clubs were of course delighted as they were not to lose players at the business end of the season which had been the case when travel to Australia had been undertaken by sea. Equally as important was the players would be home in time to take part in pre-season training rather than when the season had begun.

Those with a little more foresight saw problems particularly for the players themselves. Most of the players were to finish a season which would see them play in the region of forty odd games. They were then to board an aircraft and four days later many carrying injuries arrive in Australia and be expected to play again. Some argued that the sea voyage served two great purposes, firstly it allowed the players to re-charge the batteries and allow injuries to heal. Secondly it allowed the tour party to 'gel'. All tour parties were made up of players from different clubs and whilst they regularly played against each other they never played together as a team.

As we shall see later these two factors were to greatly affect the tourists once they arrived in the Antipodes. Another issue that was aired by some in the press was that of players ending the season in temperate conditions and soft grounds and a week later playing on the bone hard pitches and hot temperatures in Sydney. There was also one other factor which was to have its effect and that was as was mentioned earlier the twelve-man selection committee appointed to decide the makeup of the squad. The first job however was to appoint the two tour managers Hector Rawson from the Hunslet club and

Tom Hesketh from Wigan. That done the process of tour selection could begin.

A number of trial matches were arranged the first to be played at Leeds on the 24th February 1954. Even before the trial the selectors were hit by injuries and illness to players initially selected for the trial. The result was a number of changes and switching of positions occurred. When the game was completed it became apparent to the selectors and pundits in the press that there was no problem with the forwards. Quite the reverse was the case the problem being just who to leave out. The same could not be said for the situation with regards to the wingmen and more importantly the standoff position a critical one on the hard Aussie grounds.

The Chairman of Selectors was quoted as saying:-

"We aren't worried about forwards at all. But after wings our big problem is at stand-off half."

The incumbent stand-off was Barrow's Willie Horne but he was not in the best form. He had opened a sports shop in the town and was worried about the venture this had affected his play on the field. During the trial while he did a few very clever things he was in the main well contained by the Leeds standoff Gordon Brown.

The other intriguing contest was that between the Saints centre Duggie Greenall and the relative newcomer to the game from the Leeds club Welshman Lewis Jones. In the trial by clever footwork the Welshman repeatedly beat the Saints man and whilst his inexperience was shown by the way the likes of Ernie Ashcroft sold him a dummy he did his tour claims no harm. He also kicked four goals from seven attempts. By far the most impressive back on the field was Phil Jackson the twenty-one year old army trainee. Time after time he surged passed defenders with both power and a swerve. He seemed to be in every attack for his side.

The only wingman to impress out of the four on the field was Frank Castle. On one occasion he swept seventy yards down the field for a try, sadly it was the one and only time he touched the ball. The selectors really did have a problem in deciding on a set of back that they could send to Australia to defend the Ashes. All eyes were focused now on the second and final trial scheduled for Swinton on 10th March.

The selectors sprung a surprise by recalling the former international standoff Dickie Williams for the game. The two teams were:-

Whites

E. Cahill (Rochdale) B. Norburn (Swinton) D. Froggart (Wakefield) E. Gibson (Workington) D. Rose (Huddersfield) R. Williams (Hunslet) A. Burnell (Hunslet) D. Naughton (Warrington) A. Ackerley

(Halifax) D. Wilcox (Rochdale) B. Watts (York) G. Parsons (St. Helens) D. Valentine (Huddersfield)

Reds

G.Moses (St. Helens) A Turnbull (Leeds) A Naughton (Warrington) A. Davis (Oldham) T. O'Grady (Oldham) R. Price (Warrington) G. Helme (Warrington) E. Slevin (Huddersfield) A. Wood (Leeds) J. Henderson (Workington) G. Gunney (Hunslet) J. Parker (Barrow) H. Street (Wigan)

It would seem the selectors had seen enough from the forwards in the first trial to take a look at other players. In the backs they opted for combinations to see if that would solve their dilemma. The two sets of half backs were club combinations, for the Whites the Hunslet pair for the Reds the Warrington pair. The half back considered by many to be a shoo in for selection was the Huddersfield player Billy Banks. Unfortunately, he suffered a knee injury and was unable to play in the trial or the cup tie for his club the Saturday before the trial. With the injury his chances were scuppered unless the two scrum halves selected did not perform well. In an effort to solve the wing problem the selectors gave Terry O'Grady a second chance but this time paired him with his club centre Alan Davies. O'Grady still only nineteen had already earned an England cap while just seventeen years old. The three other wingers new to the trials were given an opportunity to press their claim for selection.

With the trials under way in England the Australian media were beginning to speculate as to just who would or would not make the tour party. One player under the microscope was the Leigh second row forward Charles Pawsey. It was claimed that Pawsey was suffering a slump in form that was such the club were considering dropping him for the cup tie against Leeds. Leeds won the game and Pawsey did little to impress. The media put him in the same category as Willie Horne the Barrow skipper who was also in a slump and it was felt would not make the tour party. All of the speculation came to an end the day after the final trial when on the 11th March the tour party was revealed to the media.

There were many new faces in the party announced on that Thursday and one or two old ones left the international scene. As predicted Willie Horne missed out on selection while Dave Valentine whose omission from the 1950 tour party had caused an outcry was in this time. Only four players were selected to make their second tour down under. Williams, Ashcroft and Cunliffe from the backs gained selection and Ken Traill from the forwards. The full squad was:-

R. Williams (Hunslet) captain, E. Ashcroft (Wigan) vice-captain, E. Cahill (Rochdale), J.Cunliffe (Wigan)

W.J.Boston (Wigan), A.Turnbull (Leeds), D. Greenall (St.Helens), P.B. Jackson (Barrow), L. Jones (Leeds), Frank Castle (Barrow), T. O'Grady (Oldham), R. Price (Warrington), G. Helme (Warrington), A. Burnell Hunslet), J. Henderson (Workington), A. Prescott (St.Helens), T. Harris (Hull), J. Bowden (Huddersfield), T. McKinney (Salford), J. Wilkinson (Halifax), B. Briggs (Huddersfield), G. Gunney (Hunslet), C. Pawsey (Leigh), Nat Silcock (Wigan), K. Traill (Bradford), D. Valentine (Huddersfield).

There were more than one or two surprises in the tour party not least that of Billy Boston who had made only a handful of appearances for his Wigan club. Such was the dearth of wingmen even though he had not played in the trial games he was in the party. As the Aussie press stated Boston was to be the first ever coloured player to tour Australia with an English touring side. The selectors also decided that the nineteen year old Oldham wingman O'Grady was to make the trip. Lewis Jones the Leeds centre would in fact be making his second tour of Australia having gone to the country with the British Lions rugby union party in 1950.

There was another player making a second trip down under, this time in much happier circumstances. The Hunslet scrum half Alf 'Ginger' Burnell had served in the navy during World War 2. He had served as a submariner on board HMS Spiteful and had been involved in the search for the Gneisenau and Scharnhorst in the Atlantic and Norwegian Fjords and had been seconded to the Unite States Task Force that was based in Australasia and involved in the blockade of Japan The submarine was based in Freemantle in Western Australia. Hopefully on the tour he would get a better view of the country than he got looking through a periscope!

The Wigan forward Nat Silcock would emulate his father in gaining tour selection his father touring in 1932 and 1936. The tour party while referred to as England was really a Great Britain side as there were nineteen Englishmen, four Welshmen, two Scots and an Irishman in the party.

The tour selection was however, not without its critics those in favour and those against particular players. The great Warrington wingman Brian Bevan thought that Frank Castle the Barrow wingman would prove to be a star of the tour. Former Aussie forward Arthur Clues expressed the opinion that Lewis Jones and Billy Boston would develop into a class combination, how right he was. Clues went on to say that with the experience his countrymen had gained on the 1952 tour to England they should be able to trounce the tourists.

Former tourist Gus Risman chipped in with his twopen'th as it were stating he was surprised that Gunney and

Briggs had gained selection in the second row as both he felt were inexperienced. He also expressed doubt about the winger Turnbull being able to stand up to what the Aussies would throw at him. As he said 'he is prone to show his injuries.' Risman's words were to prove prophetic as the tour progressed for Turnbull was to play only two games on the tour.

It was in the half backs that the greatest controversy occurred. It was claimed in the press that cross voting amongst the twelve-man selection committee had resulted in the exclusion of Kielty at the expense of Burnell. Even more bizarrely some selectors made the extraordinary claim that the trial referee who was from Warrington had throughout the final trial game favoured the Warrington halfbacks Price and Helme. This had given a false impression of Helme's merit by allowing illegalities that would be penalised down under! There is little doubt that within the selection committee there were cliques that favoured one player over another or one club over another. Or even a Lancashire player over a Yorkshire player. With hindsight the biggest criticism perhaps of these divisions was that it led to better combinations of players not being selected.

The other problem involved Dickie Williams who had left the field in the trial at the end of the game holding his jaw. It was an injury he felt would preclude his selection particularly as the early diagnosis was that he had suffered a broken cheekbone. In spite of this he was selected for the tour. Williams was to have an operation on the cheekbone and would not play again until he landed in Australia. It was an extra-ordinary decision when you think that the tourists were to play their first game two days after arriving in Sydney. However, it does give an insight as to just how the selectors viewed the problematical stand-off position.

With the tour selection over the game domestically could then continue. The two county cup competitions culminated in Bradford Northern overcoming Hull by a score of 7-2. On the other side of the Pennines St. Helens beat their fierce rivals Wigan by 16-8. In the League it was really four clubs that were to dominate and they finished in the top four spots namely Halifax with 62 points, Warrington with 61 points, St. Helens with 58 points and Workington also with 58 points.

The top two clubs had also battled their way through the Challenge Cup final at Wembley on the 1st May. Before that game both clubs had also won through to meet each other in a battle for the Championship via the top four play-off system. Halifax had overcome Workington 18-7 and Warrington beat St. Helens 11-0. All was set for the season ending finale when the two teams would meet twice in a week. Sadly, circumstances prevailed against that and served up an even bigger treat for the fans.

When the two teams walked out onto the turf of Wembley Stadium on Saturday the 1st May it was a fitting match up. Both teams had finished up first and second on the league table and were now to play for the Challenge Cup. The game turned out to be an anticlimax for both teams and a headache for the League authorities. At the end of the game the two teams could not be separated and the 4-4 score line meant that a replay had to be hastily arranged. Little did anyone know that the outcome of that decision would turn out to be an historic occasion.

On the following Wednesday the two teams meet again this time at Bradford's Odsal Stadium. As kick-off approached the streams of supporters at each and every turnstile was over whelming and many people tired of waiting found spots to climb over the fencing to gain entry to the ground. The official number for those in attendance was given as over 102,000 but many felt the attendance was even greater. Certainly, it was a record attendance for a rugby league game anywhere in the world. The spectators witnessed Warrington get the better of their Yorkshire rivals 18-4.

With that competition sorted out it was then on to Maine Road Manchester on the Saturday 8th May were once again the two clubs would do battle this time for the Championship. A crowd of over 36,500 turned out to see the game and many thousands more watch the game on television via BBC's Grandstand programme. The result was yet again another win for Warrington in a closely fought contest coming out on top 8-7. The other point of note during the season involved the Warrington wingman Brian Bevan who became the games top try scorer when he surpassed the 446 tries scored by the Saints wingman Alf Ellaby.

With that game the season was officially at an end but the tour was about to begin as the players were to fly out of the country on the 14th May just six days later and were due to land in Sydney on the 17th May. Each and every player was coming off a long season which had seen most play in excess of thirty-six games. Now they were to start all over again with just the briefest of respites.

There was however just one niggling little doubt in the minds of the pundits in the press and the game with regard to the makeup of the tour party. It had surfaced on the Wednesday 27 April at Bradford when the English had met the French. While England had won the encounter 17-7 the performance was less than pleasing. Only the young centre Jackson seemed to perform to a standard expected. Not only did he score a try but he also made one for Boston and one for Briggs. Lewis Jones had a torrid time against his opposite number but did kick four goals.

The match was an opportunity for those going to Australia to 'gel' but that did not happen. The conflicts within the selection committee that favoured players rather than combinations of players for the tour were plain for all to see. Too often the handling was bad and when openings were made players tended to hold onto the ball rather than passing. The other problem the selectors had was concerning Burnell, at the beginning of April he had suffered a dislocated shoulder and missed the international against France. He was ordered to see a specialist to ascertain if he was fit to tour and Banks and Kielty were put on standby should he fail the fitness test. The game did not auger well for what was to come and sadly proved to be prophetic in terms of what would happen on the tour.

CHAPTER THREE

As the players arrived at the airport on that Friday morning 14th May, many were still carrying bumps, bruises and injuries from the season just past. The tour Captain Dickie Williams had successfully come through the operation to repair his broken cheek bone but had not pulled a boot on in anger since the final trial game back in March. They were now to be on board an aircraft for around three days. If all went to plan they would arrive in Sydney on the following Monday the 17th May and were due to play Western Division two days later! It was not the best start for any tour.

While all of this was happening in England, over in Australia once the tour party was officially announced the press launched into an intensive and concerted hate campaign against the Saints centre, Duggie Greenall. The short article in the Sun of 19th March is worth looking at in full, it reads under the headline **"Welcome" for Duggie:-**

The most intensive 'hate' campaign in Rugby League history will meet English Test tourist Duggie Greenall, Australian officials and players believe.

Greenall, the St Helens centre three-quarter is coolly and deliberately provocative to the point of playing 'dirty' declares today's new issue of Sporting Life.

Some Kangaroos are already talking about a welcome for Duggie with knowing looks and winks, says the article which is bluntly outspoken.

The 'hate' is expected to be quite different from the good natured banter Frenchman, Puig-Aubert aroused or even to the barracking Bumper Farrell and Ray Stehr have faced.

It really was a disgraceful article but does give some idea of the belief the Aussies had that Greenall was the bogyman to end all bogymen. Similar articles seemed to pop up in newspapers all over New South Wales and Queensland as the tourists were awaited.

As the Australian season was well under way and the date for the tourists arrival ever closer W.F. Corbett writing in the Sun on 9th April touched on issues which seem to be as relevant today as they were back then. From what he had seen of club games in Sydney during the season he concluded that beating the English was not really a possibility. He did raise two points which may well assist the home side when he pointed out as many in England had, that flying would not allow players to get over injuries and also, they would very quickly come into contact with the hard body damaging pitches in Australia. He implied that the decision to fly was as a result of the clubs wanting their players to leave late and arrive home early so as to be available for their clubs.

He went on to raise a number of issues with the Australian game, poor passing and handling, poor tackling and so on. He argued they have not learned to tackle man and ball as the English do. He also tried to dispel the notion players had that because they had success on the 1952 tour it did not mean success was assured. As he pointed out the advantages are always with the touring side in such matters. It was then that he made the point that is still relevant to this day when he wrote:-

'Internationals complain if they try anything they have learned abroad they are discouraged by coaches.

Coaches declare that if they favour enterprising football they are condemned by club officials.'

Were it ever different you might ask as even today the NRL play a much greater negative game than does the English game.

The Australian Board pulled out all the stops in their attempts to win back the Ashes. Their first action was to appoint Vic Hey as coach to the Australian team they also agreed to a pay rise for the international players who would now earn thirty pounds each Test for their efforts. Finally, they agreed with Vic Hey's request that the Australian team be allowed to spend the week of the game in a hotel to build team spirit and understanding.

Hey was of the opinion it was understanding between players that was the difference between the tourists and the home teams.

Hey made very clear just what his tactics were going to be in the Test series when he stated;-

'The Englishmen will beat us every time we take a risk. The style of football in club and state games is beset with risks.'

The writing was on the wall for the tourists well before they arrived. The opposition would be playing risk free defensive football and attempt to stop the visitors playing the type of game they liked to play.

They say if it is possible for something to go wrong it will and so it proved with the tourist's journey. The first leg should have been pretty straight forward a flight to Rome. Sadly, when they approached Rome it was shrouded in a thick fog and the pilot could not land. He diverted the aircraft to Nice and set back the tourists well over sixteen hours. Now instead of arriving in Sydney on the Monday morning it would be late evening or early Tuesday before they arrived. They still had to play out at Bathurst on the Wednesday.

Prior to boarding the airplane there was official business to attend to namely deciding just which team would take to the field in Bathurst for the first game of the tour.

Corbett in the Sun on the 14th published the team which was :-

Cunliffe, Boston, Jones, Ashcroft, Castle, Price, Helme, Prescott, Harris, Wilkinson, Gunney, Silcock, Traill.

Corbett had obviously done his homework for he prophetically wrote in the article;-

'Boston is a sensational right wingman who is tipped as one of the stars of the tour.
The versatile Jones who plays on the wing and fullback as well as centre. He is an outstanding goal kicker and a clever attacking player.
The second rower Silcock's father toured Australia with the 1932 and 1936 British teams.'

There was one nice little touch concerning the flight down to Sydney as the tourists adopted two little Australian children who were flying home without their parents. Erica Greentrees who was just six and her brother Michael aged nine were taken under the wings of Wilkinson, Pawsey and Henderson who were taking care of the pair and entertaining them during the long flight home. With the tourists expected at any time the newspapers were full of articles about the tourists.

One column by E.E. Christensen in the Sun on the Monday the tourists were due to land had the following:-

'One English Rugby League star who will step off the plane in Sydney tonight with no worries about finding form is foxy half back Gerry Helme. Helme left home after finding room in his trophy cabinet for the Lance B Todd Memorial Trophy, which he won in the Cup Final replay at Bradford last Wednesday week. Helme has become the first player in history to win two. He also scored in 1950.

For those who are wondering who England's Test halves will be, another tourist, Ray Price at five eight was almost as good as Helme on the day.

The two Warrington boys are early favourites for the first Test on 12th June.'

Further in his Column Christensen gives a quite illuminating insight into the crazy financial running of the game at the time. He pointed out that the gate at the Cup final played at Wembley amounted to just £29,000 of which both clubs got 10% yet the cost of renting Wembley took a big chunk. The gate at the replay at Bradford was 102,575 but receipts only came to £18,650!

It was late on the Monday evening when the aircraft carrying the players touched down at what is now Kingsford-Smith Airport at Mascot in Sydney. They were met by a milling posse of pressmen all of whom had only one thing on their minds. They simply wanted a first look at this two-headed monster that was Duggie Greenall who they fully expected to walk into the airport breathing fire. They were astonished when they saw that at twelve stone he was far from being the biggest player in the backs in fact he looked quite ordinary.

After talking with the reporters, the players were whisked off to Ormond Hall out at Vaucluse which was to be their initial headquarters when they were in Sydney. On the Tuesday after breakfast the players walked from their hotel to Woollahra Oval which was to be their training ground during the stay. That done they went into the city and laid a wreath at the Cenotaph before attending the official reception.

Over one hundred and fifty were at the reception many of them reporters who proceeded to bombard Greenall about the alleged bashing of Australians in the Test matches on the last tour of England. Duggie simple said:-

'I expect to play football.'

It was left to Corbett in his article to bring a little sense to the whole issue :-

'All this talk of bashing should cease, it has no point whatever and is merely provocative. Greenall should be allowed to play his football without any references of this kind. Referees are on the field to deal with

infringements by either side. So, forget all this regrettable discussion of retaliation.'

Sadly, that was not to be the case. As we shall see Greenall came under intense scrutiny where ever the tourists went.

The other point of interest for the reporters was the attire of the team. Not a plus four in sight and it was felt they were the best dress tour party to leave England. They were wearing special hats with a red, white and blue band, hand tailored trousers, blazers and shirts. As those making the second trip pointed out they had not forgotten the floods of the last visit so all players had a raincoat.

With the official side of things out of the way it was time to get down to business and a trip out to Bathurst to play Western Districts. There were a number of changes to the team announced before the team left home namely Ashcroft was out and Greenall was in. The team for the first match of the tour at the Sports Ground in Bathurst was:-

Cunliffe, Boston, Greenall, Jones, Castle, Jackson, Burnell, Henderson, McKinney, Bowden, Silcock, Gunney, Traill.

The loose forward Traill was to have the honour of captaining the side. The tour could now truly be said to be on.

CHAPTER FOUR

Just two days after landing in Sydney the team to play Western Districts boarded a bus bound for Bathurst. It was to be the first of twenty games to be played in Australia that had been agreed to by the Rugby League Council and the Australian Board of Control over a year earlier. The full itinerary for the Australian leg of the tour was:-

19 May	Western Division	Bathurst
22 May	Newcastle	Newcastle
26 May	Riverina	Wagga-Wagga
30 May	Southern and Monaro district	Wollongong
5 June	NSW	Sydney
12 June	Australia	Sydney
14 June	Brisbane	Brisbane
19 June	Queensland	Brisbane
20 June	Wide Bay	Maryborough
23 June	Mackay	Mackay
27 June	North Queensland	Townsville
30 June	Central Queensland	Rockhampton
3 July	Australia	Brisbane
4 July	Toowoomba	Toowoomba
7 July	Northern NSW	Grafton
10 July	NSW	Sydney
17 July	Australia	Sydney
18 August	NSW	Sydney
21 August	Southern Districts	Canberra
23 August	Newcastle Coalfields	Grafton

New Zealand - Leg

21 July	Whangarei	Auckland Maori
24 July	Auckland	New Zealand
27 July	Wellington	Wellington
31 July	Greymouth	New Zealand
4 August	Dunedin	South Island
7 August	Christchurch	Canterbury
9 August	New Plymouth	North Island
11 August	Hamilton	South Auckland
14 August	Auckland	New Zealand
16 August	Auckland	Auckland

As 3.00pm. approached the two teams took to the field on a cool still afternoon and around 8,000 spectators cheered both teams onto the pitch. The tourists had not had the best preparation as the bus arrived late in Bathurst so the players had little time after lunch before heading for the Sports Ground. The tourists had made a few changes from that published earlier and the players that took to the field were:-

Cunliffe, Boston, Greenall, Jones, O'Grady, Jackson, Burnell, Henderson, McKinney, Bowden, Silcock, Briggs, Traill.

Most had come to see the 'devil' himself, Duggie Greenall, along with the new wing sensation the press had been writing up, Billy Boston, they were not disappointed.

It was the centre Lewis Jones who opened the scoring on the tour for the visitors when he slotted over a penalty. The first try was claimed by Burnell following a magical sleight of hand by the stand-off Jackson that set Boston on a powerful run infield. As he was tackled Burnell was on hand to take the pass and shoot through for the try. Nat Silcock had the honour of being the first visitor to be cautioned by the referee when he and the opposition player Potter had a bit of an argument. In the end the game was won easily enough.

There was no doubting the man of the match for all agreed that belonged to the Welshman Billy Boston who was at time almost unstoppable. William Corbett wrote of him:-
'Boston exhibited outstanding pace, determination, a swerve and sidestep tacklers seemingly unable to keep a grasp of him. To them he seemed to possess some phenomenal power of elusiveness.'

Boston crossed for two tries one following a sixty-yard run and the second even better after out pacing the opposition in a seventy-yard sprint to the whitewash. Both tries were without doubt the product of great passes from his centre Greenall. The result was a pleasing win by 29-11, the tourist's points coming from Boston two tries, O'Grady try, Burnall try and Silcock try. Jones showed just how valuable he was going to be on the tour by slotting seven goals during the afternoon.

It was not all good news for the English for as in previous tours the referee or more precisely his interpretation of the rules, particularly appertaining to the play the ball where at odds with those held by the players. The other problem was that whilst there had been great displays from individual players the team had lacked cohesion and understanding. That was to be expected given the preparation the team had but against better opposition it could become a big problem. The problems surrounding the play the ball were tackled immediately by the two managers as we shall see.

The day after the match Corbett gave a reasoned assessment of the game and in his opinions were:-

'Boston is one of the greatest attacking wingmen I have ever seen from England.
Terry O'Grady's speed and determination on the left flank: some of his runs were reminiscent of the mighty Stanley Smith.
Phil Jackson's brilliance at five eighth his weaving runs through openings and skill in turning defence into attack.
Jones craftsmanship at centre.
The all-round quality of Greenall his defence and his slashing runs in attack. On yesterday's display

Greenall is a greatly maligned performer. I watched him closely. He played hard certainly but Rugby League isn't an exhibition of croquet. There wasn't an act by Greenall at which anybody could quibble. He was most earnest in protestations yesterday that he does nothing illegal but merely plays the game hard as it should be.

As for second rowers Silcock and Briggs and front rowers Jim Henderson, Tom McKinney and Jim Bowden when they get into gear it would be gentler playing around with a freight train.'

Corbett did however make the point that cohesion was lacking in the pack in general and the team as a whole.

The issue of the play the ball was tackled by the tour managers immediately after the game when they requested that a top referee be allowed to visit the players. There the referee could officiate at a practice game with the emphasis being on getting players to play to the Australian interpretation. The Australian Board appointed Darcy Lawler who was considered the number one referee in Sydney to visit the English camp. It would seem the main disagreement in this area was that the Australians were allowed to stand up in line with the dummy half where as in England all kept behind the dummy half. The English interpretation does not allow players to form a shied to obstruct the opposition also it allows more open play from the ruck.

Referee Lawler felt after working for an afternoon with the Englishmen that they were playing the ball correctly. Corbett also formed the opinion that in his view both sides were guilty of incorrectly playing the ball at times. As on previous tours it was a problem that was not going to go away and the team would need to correct any faults quickly. Simply because just three days later they were to travel up to Newcastle and face a far more difficult opposition than Western District.

The managers were under no illusion with regard to the difficulties they faced in Newcastle and decided that a near Test side would be needed to win the game. Accordingly the team selected was:-

Cahill, Turnbull, Greenall, Ashcroft, Castle, Price, Helme, Wilkinson, Harris, Prescott, Pawsey, Briggs, Valentine.

The good folks of Newcastle felt that their boys were more than capable of beating the tourists and turned up in record numbers to the Sports Ground on the Saturday afternoon. When the two team took to the field the record attendance was given as 22,825. The tour managers were pleased that such a crowd had generated a gate of £3,880 they always had an eye on the finances.

When play began the English started by throwing the ball about as they had in the first game. The home side did exactly the opposite, they were content to play tight and keep the ball in the pack. It was Helme that was to break open the home defence when he worked a run around with the skipper Ashcroft. He then dummied his way through the defence and fed Castle who did the rest out pacing the Newcastle players to score under the posts.

A penalty goal from Cahill who had converted the try gave the tourists a 7-0 lead. Then the referee began to influence the game by making strange decisions. In truth he seemed to baffle both sides but the home players kept their cool and stuck to the game plan. The visitors on the other hand began arguing with the referee and their frustration saw play become quite rough and disjointed. The Newcastle players took full advantage and Banks scored a try which closed the score.

It then fell to the other wingman for the visitors Turnbull to take a hand in proceedings. He picked up a loose ball virtually on his own line and powered down the touchline the length of the field to score in the corner for an unconverted try. The home side were keeping themselves in the game by converting penalties and continuing to play the game tight. They frustrated the English pack and starved the backs of the ball. Late in the game from yet another penalty the Newcastle team took the lead 11-10 and protected it to the end of the game.

Photograph courtesy of Terry Williams at the NRL Museum

The tourists had lost and more worrying was the
disjointed performance they had put up in the second
half. While players were performing well as individuals
they were simply not 'gelling' as a team and it showed. It
did not auger well for the rest of the tour. It was true the
referee had not helped their cause but then he did little to

assist Newcastle. At times the large crowd made their feelings known and actually invaded the pitch before the game was at an end. There was no doubt that concern in the camp was the best way to describe the mood. But there was little time to brood as Riverina awaited them on the following Wednesday.

In the Sun newspaper on the Monday the writer E.E. Christensen gave the Aussie selectors a tip on just how they could win back the Ashes:-

'If Australia's rugby league selectors can dig up a player with shark-like features they will have no fears about handling English star Duggie Greenall. Greenall dreads sharks, breathes a sign of relief every time he has safely crossed a stretch of water. All the way to Newcastle by bus on Saturday he kept inquiring whether each patch of water crossed was shark infested.
Yesterday he attended Bondi Iceberg's welcome at Bondi Baths and acted as lookout as Geoff Gunney, Brian Briggs and Jack Wilkinson as they swam outside the baths. Greenall refused all requests to take a dip.
"I've never seen a one legged three quarter yet and I'm not letting sharks make one of me."
Later it was suggested that there were plenty Sunday's on which Greenall could try the waters.
"Aye and the sharks will still be waiting." he replied.

Greenall entertained the big crowd of sportsmen present by an excellent rendition of two Al Jolson numbers.'

Even at this early stage in the tour a number of factors were quite apparent. Firstly, the Aussies had worked out that playing their normal style of open football would simply be playing into the tourist's hands as they had superior backs. The way to beat the visitors was to starve them of the ball and to do that they needed to play in the forwards. The second thing was that the team had no time to 'gel' a long season, short flight and attempts to give all players a game meant no continuity was possible. The third factor was that teams the tourists were to meet in major cities if the Newcastle game was to be repeated were going to attempt to 'soften up' the visitors. It augured for a difficult tour and so it turned out to be.

With two games played and a win and a loss record the tourists were looking to get back on track. The next game was to be played in Wagga-Wagga against Riverina and while it was expected that the win would be easily achieved the managers were taking no chances. They named a very strong side for the match on the Wednesday and included the tour skipper for the first time:-

Cahill, Turnbull, Jackson, Ashcroft, O'Grady, Williams, Helme, Henderson, McKinney, Bowen, Gunney, Pawsey, Valentine.

The decision was made that only sixteen players would travel out to Wagga for the game the rest would remain in Sydney and train. On the Monday afternoon for the first time since arriving the players had a good training session which went on for almost two hours. The hope was that players would get a better understanding of each other's play. They needed to because while Riverina may be considered an easy game the upcoming match against Sydney would be anything but that.

On the Wednesday as was expected the tourists won relatively easily by 36-26, that said it was not a good performance. Once again it was individual brilliance on the part of players rather than a team effort that won the day. Equally worrying was that the opposition were allowed back into the game in the latter part of the second half. It was only 10-6 at half time after Pawsey and Ashcroft had crossed for tries that Cahill had converted.

Early in the second spell McKinney crashed over for another converted try taking the score out to 15-6. Gunney then went in at the corner for an unconverted try making the score 18-6. An interception by Jackson made it 21-6 and the tourists seemingly cruising. That all changed suddenly when Turnbull was injured and was taken from the ground by ambulance. The injury unsettled the rhythm of the visitors and the home side took full advantage.

With the home side earlier seemingly at sixes and sevens they suddenly produced some excellent play and cut the tourist defence to shreds scoring four unanswered tries to actually go in front 26-21. Try as they may the Englishmen could not get across the try line as dropped passes thwarted them time after time. It was left to Jackson to sort out the problem when after good play he put Gunney in for his second try and Cahill's goal levelled the scores with just five minutes left in the match. With the home side tiring Ashcroft broke from inside his twenty-five yard area and once clear fed O'Grady who sped away to score under the posts. Burnell just on time crossed for a converted try which gave the score line a lopsided appearance.

It was not a good performance and one that was increasingly worrying the managers as the game should have been put to bed at 21-6 rather than having to pull it out of the fire in the last minutes of the game. The injury to Turnbull was assessed and turned out to be not as serious as first suspected being only a torn muscle. The managers however had more problems to solve particularly with the press.

The Greenall saga had continued to follow the tourists wherever they travelled and the radio people in particular were constantly wanting to talk to Greenall and discuss the events of two years ago when the Aussies were in England. Alan Hulls writing in the Sun on that Wednesday gives us an insight into the events at the time:-

'First was that the English managers avoided a possible building-up of the Greenall nonsense by banning radio interviews by the players. The bogey of "Killer" Greenall was beginning to reach ridiculous proportions and to be a real threat to any hopes of an harmonious tour. Managers Rawson and Hesketh were wise to keep him in the background at such a delicate period of the tour - even if his radio interview had been publicised.'

The problems off the field with reporters continually harping on about Greenall was not what was wanted particularly as the tour was not going that well on the field. The language used by the reporters was not helping the situation rather it was building up the Greenall factor. I suppose the managers took the only action open to them by simply banning Greenall from speaking. Had Greenall been allowed to speak it would have been pouring more fuel on the fire, better to stop all players from speaking on the radio. Equally the managers could have for their part launched a more vigorous defence of

Greenall than they appear to have done. They adopted a least said soonest mended approach. With the players back in Sydney preparations got under way for what was considered to be the toughest encounter of the tour to date.

With the game against Sydney fast approaching the managers named a fifteen-man squad for the match selecting three three quarters in Ashcroft Greenall and Jones along with three props, Henderson, Bowden and Wilkinson. Boston and Castle were restored to the flanks and Williams retained his place in the side with Cunliffe replacing Cahill. Interestingly Corbett writing of the game at Wagga was convinced that the tourists were playing to a preconceived plan designed to give little or nothing away to the watching Aussie coach Vic Hey. As Corbett said it was the only way one could explain the alternating nature of play particularly in the second half by the visitors.

On the Saturday at the Cricket Ground just short of 51,000 supporters went through the turn stiles and watch a game that was thrilling from start to finish. The visitors decided that it would be prudent to go into the game with a good goal kicker and so dropped Castle from the side and replaced him with Greenall allowing Lewis Jones to play in the centre. The first twenty minutes of the game saw the home side take a seven nil lead and the tourists were struggling to get into the match. They slowly got to grips with the pace of the game and two goals from Jones and a try from Williams levelled the scores at 7-7.

From that point on the lead constantly changed hands but the tourists were always on the back foot. They did take the lead at 17-14 but it was the last time they would be in that position. In the end the superior pace of the home side saw them come out on top by 32-25. Once again, the tourists had relied on individual brilliance rather than good team work and great combinations. It was all rather worrying particularly as the first Test was fast approaching.

On the Sunday following the Sydney game the tourists took to the field yet again this time down at the Wollongong Show Ground to play the Southern and Monaro District. It was a game that saw the visitors come away with a 17-17 draw. The game was not without controversy once again and yet again Greenall in the firing line not for the first time as we have see. The tourists put in a lack lustre performance that was disjointed and uncoordinated. At times player would make a half break only to find no one in support. The tackling at times also was not of the standard expected of a touring side.

The one redeeming feature was that a record crowd of 15,435 generated a gate of £2,580. Given that the tourists dominated the scrums with all the possession they should have won the game going away but all too often fell foul of the referee. He constantly penalised them for indiscretions at the play the ball. The local reporter in the Illawarra newspaper felt that the duel between Harry Wells and Duggie Greenall was a feature of the game, that was until in his words:-

'Geenall sickened Wells in the second half with a flying tackle.'

Late in the game with the score at 17-14 to the English the home side had the opportunity to win the game. They scored a try out wide but the conversion attempt went wide.

Christensen writing in the Sun said of Greenall:-

'League centres playing opposite Greenall all need a third eye in the side of their heads. This was proved at Wollongong yesterday when the much discussed Englishman knocked out Harry Wells with a high tackle, in which he leapt into the air and crashed Wells to the ground. Greenall's plan is to stand out wide from the man and as the opponent turns to take the ball from his team mate inside, Greenall goes in from the blind spot. Wells said this was the move used by Greenall to iron out Noel Hazzard in England during the last Test series. Wells promised not to fall for it again.'

The two managers must have despaired at reading the article as far from calming the situation Christensen was stoking up the fire not only with supporters of the game but also future opponents who may well face the Saints man. It really was a disgraceful article from the Aussie reporter as the tackle was not penalised by the referee and Greenall had done nothing illegal. It does show however the hysteria generated by the press around Greenall on this tour. Once again the managers did not take the opportunity to defend the player.

Far more worrying was the fact that the Test was fast approaching and there were very few signs that the touring team was actually beginning to 'gel' into just that- a team. The managers recognised the problem but were at a loss as to just how to solve it. Corbett again writing in the Sun hit the nail on the head when at the beginning of June he wrote:-

'But the tourists have not yet welded on the field as an effective unit. They perform some fine things and then others that are thoroughly inglorious. They need moulding into a team of understanding. There are too many bits and pieces - loose tackles, lack of backing up, failure to anticipate in attack. England must start winning a string of matches or public interest will lag.

At times the English have looked weary and incapable of concerted attack or defence. Observers

have been making very unfavourable comparisons between this team and English teams of the past. England commit fundamental errors on the field yet have some notable players. But unless they achieve teamwork and tightness these men will remain individualists. There are too many positional faults.'

It was easy enough to identify such problems but not so easy to correct them.

The team spent the week preparing for the game on Saturday 5th June, against New South Wales and the managers put on a brave face at least to the press. They promised the team would play harder on the Saturday and play like an English team should. The problem they faced however was should they keep experimenting with the side or play the strongest side they could on the Saturday. The players in the tour party were in truth all very good individually and so competition for Test places was fierce the question was which thirteen were the best players for the upcoming Test match.

As the game came closer the famous Aussie cricketer Keith Miller wrote in his column a piece which is as relevant today as it was when he wrote it in 1954:-

'Did you sight the signboard at the Sydney Cricket Ground this week? It announced that Great Britain will play New South Wales at the SCG on Saturday. Even this high falutin' piece of phraseology must look bewildering to rugby leagues most rabid fans. After all the English team has for many years been known as England not Great Britain. Even the accepted name of England applied to rugby league teams is a most dubious one. Rugby League is played only in two counties in Northern England. But perhaps we shouldn't dwell too long on that subject for we are not much better calling ourselves the Australian Rugby League team. Unlike tennis, cricket and athletics which are nation-wide sports rugby league is played only in New South Wales and Queensland. All the other states are dominated by Australian Rules which is played more extensively in Australia than any other code. It would be much nearer the mark if the League Test advertisements read North of England v A Combined NSW-Q team.'

We seem to have made little if any progress in that direction in the last sixty odd years in either country.

If the two managers felt that they were forever fighting off criticism from the press over Greenall and their perceived poor performances on the field along with the reasons for those performances. In truth they seemed to have adopted a typically English stance of stoic silence with regard to the press. What they did not know was that a veritable tornado of criticism in another area was gathering power and it was of their own making. For now, they had a game to prepare for and one that really needed to be won if the tour was not to be derailed. They were to face New South Wales and the rugby league public were looking on to see if the tourists could turn around the tour. They had played five games and won only two it was far from being the start they would have wanted.

At the Cricket Ground on that Saturday around 53,000 packed into the ground to see the game. Ashcroft won the toss and as the game started it seemed all the managers had promised was about to come to fruition. Sadly, the tourists flattered to deceive and after a bright opening passage of play lapsed back in the ragged performance that seemed to have permeated performances during the tour to date. They did take the lead but it was through a penalty goal by Cahill the full back. That was quickly cancelled out by the home side.

While the English forwards were playing much tougher than in previous games the superior speed of the home side was clear to see. The crowd had a bit of a laugh at Frank Castle's expense as the game was stopped while a bandage was taken on to the field and used to hold his shorts up. On the fifteen- minute mark the tourists launched a dazzling attack, Jackson, Greenall, Helme and Ashcroft combined to free Castle. He needed no encouragement to speed to the corner for an unconverted try.

The play augured well for the visitors and showed just what they really were capable of producing. The other marked change to previous game was a willingness to keep kicking the ball deep into enemy territory thus stopping full back Churchill from coming into the attack. The home side closed the gap with a penalty and as half time was approaching took the lead with a well worked try. Worse was to follow when Holman broke away and scored another try. All the good work of the first half by the tourists was undone and the home side went into the dressing rooms 10-5 in the lead.

In the second half the referee had his hands full containing the forwards as tempers began to flare up. From yet another penalty Churchill increased the lead to 12-5. Worse still was to follow as the home side crossed for a converted try and with the score now at 17-5 the game was quickly slipping away. Now the pace of the home side came to the fore and they began to run the tourists ragged. It was inevitable that further scoring would occur and it was the home side that combined to take the score out to 22-5.

Inevitable with the game seemingly won the Sydney side took their foot off the gas and the Barrow wingman Castle crossed for a try. Castle was not done and produced the try of the game late in the match. Getting the ball sixty-five yards out he beat all in front of him to complete his hat trick by scoring in the corner. He bamboozled the full back Churchill with a change of pace and brought the house down as he scored.

It was too little too late from the Englishmen and once again it was the lack of team work that had let them down. Players had performed well individually but could not combine individual flair with team effort. As expected the press had a field day and stated that the first Test just a week away was a foregone conclusion. It was not a question of would Australia win but rather by how many. Something needed to be done and something drastic at that. The two managers sat down and planned to do just that. It was obvious to all that the tourists were a team of champion players but were always beaten by a champion team. They had individuals that could turn a game against most teams but in the games that mattered they were always stifled and starved of quick possession. The question was a simple one what was to be done?

The first Test was almost upon them and the results to date were poor to say the least. When the managers read the newspapers on Monday once again poor old Greenall was coping it. In his column Christensen wrote of the trials that Harry Wells the Aussie centre had faced, appendicitis, then a broken hand which then developed boils. He then discovered he was slightly deaf from an injury sustained the previous year. If that were not enough Christensen wrote:-

'On his home ground at Wollongong yesterday week he was ko'd by Greenall, who repeated the performance on Saturday and broke Wells' jaw into the bargain.'

It seemed the press were not going to let up on the Saints centre but the two managers once more failed to come to the defence of the player. They would make a decision that would take their mind and that of the press off Greenall. Before that in the same issue of the Sun Corbett had a dig at the players stating there were lots of loose ends for the team to correct. He also expressed the opinion the players could not last the eighty minutes either from a lack of condition or staleness from coming off a long season back home with no rest. Corbett was certainly pulling no punches but there was little the players or managers could say as his comments were spot on the mark.

The only good news for the embattled tourists was the fact that the gate receipts were more than healthy in spite of the results on the field. Hector Rawson did add that the cost of staging this tour were the greatest ever faced by the Rugby League in England. He referred to the costs as being colossal. Both he and Hesketh were about to add to those costs as was revealed the following day. They released the fifteen that were to contest the first Test on the Saturday and missing from the list were tour skipper Dickie Williams and Duggie Greenall. Both were injured Greenall suffering from damaged ribs and a head injury while Williams had a gash on his head.

It was also revealed that the players had been placed on a 6.00pm curfew and were not to leave the hotel after that time. It was an action that was to cause resentment among the players who felt they were being treated very much like naughty children. What the two managers did not want to see was an article in the Sun that same day stating that they had approached the former Australian Test player Ray Stehr to coach the tourists. This they denied but Stehr was adamant this was the case. Stating:-

'I had a long discussion with the managers on Sunday morning when an English pressman was also present. Mr Rawson was most anxious that I should accept the position. And was so insistent that I promised to give him an answer on Sunday evening.'

Whether the approach was true or not was of no consequence as it was not to be Stehr that was appointed to coach the visitors but another former Aussie player Ross McKinnon that was appointed to the job. By doing so Hesketh and Rawson had effectively poked a stick into a hornet's nest. The following day the newspapers were full of comments from officials of the New South Wales Rugby League as well as the Australian Board. None more vociferous than Harry Flegg the Board President who labelled the decision a disgrace and lowering the prestige of Rugby League. He went on to say:-

'I cannot understand the action of English officials. If they consider they are going bad, why don't they face up to the music without enlisting the aid of an Australian coach.'

Rawson's response was typically English saying that he had received no official complaints and if there were complaints there was a correct time and place to make them. It was an approach he previously had taken and was to adopt consistently at every controversy that occurred during the tour. To the onlookers though it smacked of panic from the tourists as the first Test loomed. If Hesketh and Rawson thought the whole affair was simply a storm in a teacup they were in for a rude awakening when they saw the response from officials back home in England. At the games Annual General Meeting many voiced their criticism of the two manager's decision.

The article in the Sun on the 10th June pointed out that Rawson had favoured appointing an Australian coach even before the party left England. The reason given by Rawson for the appointment namely the problem around the play the ball area was also shot down. The Council Chairman Mr. Robinson felt that play the ball rules were clearly defined and if there was a problem with them then the two countries needed to get together and thrash out the differences. A former Council Chairman Mr. Bennett was perturbed by the actions of the managers and felt they had more than enough experience to coach the players. If they could not, then surely amongst the twenty-six players there was someone who could have done the job.

Bennett went on to say that the problems of the tour were not due to selection issues but rather by rushing the players out to Australia by air travel:-

'I have always been opposed to rushing men who have just finished nine months of hard football into another hectic season. A sea voyage would have given the men a chance to rest and get ready for an Australian campaign.'

The Chairman of selectors Bob Anderton was one who put a little better perspective on the issue when he stated that the players were not to blame. He also stated that the Australians when on tour had hired the former English forward Joe Thompson to coach them. Harry Flegg was unrepentant with regard to his remarks even though other board members disassociated themselves from his comments. Flegg stated that the English had panicked even before they had lost the first Test. It was all becoming very messy and only added to the woes of the players.

In amidst all the arguments a very important issue was lost with regard to the development of the game as the Sun carried the news that there was a plan by the tourists to abandon the last two games of the tour. The intention was to replace them by two exhibition games in the United States on the way home. The original plan was to return to Australia at the end of the New Zealand leg of the tour and now it was proposed to fly from New Zealand to California instead. There they would play a couple of exhibition games. The issue was due to be discussed by the two managers and the Australian Board. Sadly, as we now know nothing came of the proposal and once again an opportunity to establish a foothold in the States was lost by the British game. The Australian Board on the other hand a few weeks later agreed that following the World Cup in France in the October They would play two exhibition games against New Zealand in America.

(Following the World Cup competition held in France in October of 1954 the Australian and New Zealand squads flew to New York. After a few days sight seeing the teams flew on to California and prepared for the first exhibition game. This was to be played in Los Angeles on Friday 26th November but was cancelled due to fog and played the following day and the Australians won by 30-13 in front of just 1000 supporters. Just two days later the two teams met again

at Long Beach in California and the Aussies were again victorious winning by 28-18 in front of 4554 supporters. For more information regarding this enterprise see Appendix One)

All of the upheaval was not the best preparation for the upcoming Test a game that had now become vital to the success or failure of the tour. On that Saturday afternoon 65,884 paid to witness this first Test encounter this in spite of all the pundits predicting that the Australians would win with ease. Sadly their predictions proved correct, the two teams were:-

Australia:-
Churchill, Pidding, McCaffery, Watson, Carlson, Banks, Holman, Bull, Kearney, Hall, Provan. O'Shea, Crocker.

England:-
Cunliffe, Jones, Ashcroft, Jackson, Castle, Price, Helme, Prescott, McKinney, Wilkinson, Valentine, Silcock, Trail.

The managers made the decision to go with Jones on the wing instead of Boston. The feeling was that it would be prudent to take to the field with a proven goal kicker rather than the attacking flair of the Wigan wingman.

When the game kicked off it was the green and gold that opened the scoring when Provan crashed over for a try.

It came from a quick play the ball and a long pass from Kearney to Holman, he was able to set Hall free. Hall when about to be tackles slipped a pass to Provan who did the rest. Pidding stepped up for the simplest of conversions and incredibly put the ball wide. What followed was almost constant pressure from the home side but the visitors defence held out every attack.

As is the case when a team is soaking up so much pressure it is they that then break out and score and so it was. Traill picked up from the ruck on his own twenty-five yard line and ran out wide. He gave a reverse pass to Valentine that put him through the defensive line and he carried the ball up the middle of the field. As he approached the full back Churchill he committed him to the tackle and passed out to the supporting Silcock who had a clear run to the line of some forty yards or more. He was chased down by Pidding but as he was tackled slid over under the posts. Jones tacked on the goal and the Englishmen were in front 5-3. As the half was coming to a close O'Shea scored by the posts and Pidding goaled to put the home side in front once more. Pidding increased the lead with a great penalty goal from out wide and as the two teams went in for the break the score was 10-5 in favour of Australia. It was a case of the same old problem for the tourists a good start and then a failure to continue to the end of the half.

The tourists would have been pleased though with that score as they had soaked up a great deal of pressure and not allowed the home side to take the game away from them. They did have great problems in the dressing room with two of the forwards. The loose forward Traill had suffered a rib injury that left him struggling to play. Also, Silcock the second row had badly injured an ankle and he too was struggling. As was revealed later by the coach McKinnon if it had been anything other than a Test match neither player would have been asked to go out and play the second spell.

In spite of all the problems it was the tourists who were to score first in the second spell. From a scrum Helme and Price combined to get the ball to Jackson who slipped past his opposite number McCaffery and once clear easily beat the full back Churchill to score by the posts. Jones stepped up and levelled the scores. The lead was very quickly regained when Pidding slotted over yet another penalty. Slotted over does not do justice to Pidding's effort which was a kick from around fifty yards out and into the wind! Jones once more responded in kind when he put over a goal from off the touch line and almost on the half way line to make it 12-12.

Sadly, for the tourists once again they could not sustain the efforts, the lack of Traill and Silcock at full capacity was to prove too big a handicap. The flood gates opened and a flurry of scores took the game away from the Englishmen. Their cause was not helped when first Valentine already doing the work of Silcock and Traill as well as his own was injured. Worse was to follow when Castle the wingman was carried off with a badly gashed knee which required eight stitches and took no further part in proceedings.

As the game came to a close the score line read Australia 37 the tourists 12, it was a sombre visitor's dressing room which resembled an emergency ward. The game produced all sorts of records, a new winning margin, a new record points score by an individual with Pidding bagging nineteen with eight goals and a try. Pidding also overtook Dally Messenger's total points scored in Test matches of 43 he scoring 44.

It has to be said that the game followed the path of other games lost, namely, the visitors exhibited individual brilliance at times but were sadly lacking in team work. The home side were much fitter and faster all around the pitch and it was that which saw them take the spoils. In defence of the visitors the press made little mention of or gave consideration to the fact that the English played most of the second half with only eleven fit men. Traill and Silcock had been virtual passengers on the field and Castle the wingman had been off for a considerable time in the second half. Valentine had also suffered an injury just prior to the game slipping away from the tourists. When those facts were considered then the home side performance was not as superb as the press made it out. Neither was the tourists' performance as bad as the press made it out to be either. In truth the players would have taken a little heart from that fact realising there was really not that much between the two teams when both were at full strength.

The tourists had little time to lick their wounds as they were to leave Sydney the following day bound for Brisbane and the Queensland leg of the tour where the second Test was to be played. First, they were to meet a Brisbane side on the Monday evening in a game played under floodlights. Thankfully gone was the long over night train journey up to Queensland an airplane did the journey in around three hours.

CHAPTER FIVE

When the tourists arrived in Brisbane the two managers sought out the Queensland Secretary Ron McAuliffe and instructed him to cancel all social engagements that were not a 'must'. They were determined that the players along with the coach McKinnon would spend as much time as possible on the training field. They were not going to be found wanting in the last twenty minutes of another game on the tour. Not even the news that the Sydney Test had produced a world record gate receipt of £16,842 could soften the mood of the tourist managers.

Given that the players had just finished a tough season back home the question must be asked if the managers were adopting the right approach. The players needed to be freshened up and that was not going to happen by flogging them on the training pitch. Also, by restricting the social aspect of the tour it would not have sat well with a great many of the players. With the benefit of hind-sight a more relaxed approach may well have produced better results. However, the first Test had been lost and no matter how you wrap it up a loss is a loss.

Determined to start the Queensland leg with a win a strong team was selected to take to the field on that Monday evening. For the first time on the tour under the flood lights the team seemed to 'gel' as they took apart a Brisbane side 34-4. The home side was not the strongest it has to be said but the visitors instead of playing the ball in the ruck went on a passing spree. As the local reporter put it they 'blinded the Brisbane side with science'. The game being played under floodlights the authorities had painted four white stripes on the ball to make it easier to see. All the players seemed to be happy with that fact apart from Jones who complained he could not sight the seam of the ball when lining up kicks at goal. Then again you cannot please everyone whatever you do.

There is no doubt that the win boosted the morale of both players and managers and it seems one or two of the reporters. Certainly, Bill Corbett writing in the Brisbane Telegraph was full of praise for the players. He described their performance as:-

"The traditional England of brilliant unorthodox shock attack."

He was of the opinion that players such as Helme and Pawsey really showed just why they had gained selection. The more important notion he put forward was that should the team defeat a very strong Queensland side on the weekend then the Test series was far from over. The home side he felt would really have a fight on its hands in the second Test in Brisbane.

There was one piece of bad news from home however particularly for the managers. The elections for the Management Committee of the Northern Rugby League had been held and while Tom Hesketh had managed to hold on to his seat by the skin of his teeth, Hector Rawson was not so lucky. He had garnered only eight votes and had been voted off the committee. One can only assume that the furore that had greeted the decision to appoint an Australian coach both in Australia and back home had swayed the voting against Rawson. Also the results to date on the tour would not have sat well with many back in England.

As preparations continued for the Queensland encounter on the week end the doctor had to be called to look at Frank Castle. The knee that had been stitched was swelling up alarmingly and causing him a great deal of pain. The doctor removed four of the eight stitches in the wound to ease the swelling and hopefully the pain for Castle. In the press the mood seemed to have now switched from when Queensland beat England to if they could actually win the upcoming encounter. This seemed to stimulate public interest and a record crowd of over 30,000 was being predicted. Such was the interest that the supporters were assured in the press that they would all be able to get into the ground to see the action.

The managers were just a little concerned about the man who was to referee the game, Frank Ballard. He was on the list of referees sent to the managers in order that they may select the referee from for the second Test. Ballard was well known to the tourists as back in 1950 he had been in charge of the second Test again up in Brisbane. The home team had won the game 15-3 to level the series but Ballard had sent off Ken Gee and Tommy Bradshaw during the game. The managers were hoping that history would not repeat itself come Saturday.

Many of the Queensland reporters who watched the tourists in training were sure that they were now yards faster than when they arrived. Billy Boston was one who had attracted attention when he arrived simply because of his speed over the ground but now he was even faster. O'Grady was not far behind him and even the old stager Ashcroft appeared to be moving faster over the hard grounds in the northern state. The harder grounds did have a down side as well and a lot of the players were complaining of sore ankles. The managers requested that the grass at the ground be left long for the game so as to act as a cushion for the players.

The managers revealed that three of the players on the injured list while not selected for the Queensland game would return on the following day against Wide Bay. The three were Greenall who had suffered a rib injury and a gash to the head. Alf Burnell who had suffered an ankle injury in the game down in Wollongong and Gunney who had not played since the game out at Wagga-Wagga due to a deep-seated abscess in his thigh.

On the Saturday as predicted a record crowd arrived to watch the game and at kick off around 25,000 were in attendance. The Englishmen knew the importance of the game and dominated from the outset. The forwards in particular were tackling like demons and stifling the home forwards attacking flair. The backs had speed and strength and Boston and O'Grady caused problems each time they got the ball. With twenty minutes remaining the tourists were leading 24-19 but once more fell off the pace a little as the game was coming to an end. They did however after an exciting encounter walk from the field having achieved what they had set out to do, win. The win was closer than they would have liked at 34-32 but the win had put the whole of the tour party in a much happier mood.

The star undoubtably was Boston who blasted his way to three tries, Jones, Helme, O'Grady, Valentine and Pawsey also crossed for three pointers and Jones kicked five goals. It was a win that really set the tour back on track but there was little time for the players to enjoy the moment. At 7.00pm. following the game they were flying out of Brisbane bound for Maryborough and a game against Wide Bay on the Sunday. It was a game that proved to be of little difficulty as they won going away by 60-14. There was however the inevitable controversy during the game but this time it was the home side that caused the problem.

The rules in Queensland allowed for the substitution of injured players and although it was pointed out prior to the game that in games against the tourists such substitutions were not allowed. The coach of Wide Bay however took the decision to disregard the directive of his own authorities and when a player was injured he sent on a substitute. The Wide Bay authorities were both angry and embarrassed but the English managers made light of the act but did reiterate that their rules did not allow for substitutions.

They had bigger worries for the precautions they had taken with regard to trying to prevent ankle injuries from the bone hard pitches that of insisting players bandage their ankles was not working. They had ten players now suffering ankle injuries of varying severity, Cunliffe, Burnell, O'Grady, Silcock, Valentine, Jones, Gunney, Prescott, Briggs and Cahill had been laid low. There were still more games to be played in North Queensland and some players would have to play out of position to give others a rest.

With Wide Bay out of the way it was on to Mackay where they were due to play on the Tuesday. When they arrived at the ground they saw a fairground surrounding the place and side show barkers calling out to attract custom. The local authorities had gone all out for the game and even organised an exhibition of agricultural machinery. The pitch itself was so hard that in the curtain raiser between two schoolboy teams both side took to the field and played in bare feet! The atmosphere may well have been welcoming and friendly the game was not.

It quickly became obvious that the local referee was out of his depth and at times completely lost control of the players. Punches were thrown with great regularity and boots flew thick and fast. The official could have sent off any number of people but it was Briggs that was forced to take the long walk for an early bath. The game came to an end but sadly the farce and controversy did not. As the players left the field at the end of the game it was pointed out that there was actually still eight minutes to play but with the score at 28-7 it was decided not to take the players back out onto the field. Sadly, for the tourists it was a game that saw all the old troubles return, dropped balls, poor backing up and poor finishing and a lack of teamwork. Added to that allegations of rough and foul play were raised by members of the press.

After the game the local officials held a disciplinary meeting and took the decision ridiculous as it may seem to suspend Briggs for one game. That in itself was not unusual however, the suspension was only to come into operation if Briggs were to get sent from the field at any time during the rest of the tour irrespective of what action was taken at that time! I suppose that was typical of country football authorities at that time.

Sadly, the troubles for the tourists did not end there for after the game they were in The Mackay Hotel enjoying a beer or two with the opposition and some of the locals. Henderson, Wilkinson and Briggs were sat at the bar enjoying a beer when they were approached aggressively by three local men. The locals had apparently had more than enough of the amber nectar. One of the locals then shout out to Briggs that **'he was yellow'**. Wilkinson remonstrated with them in defence of his mate telling them not to talk like that. It was then one of the men threw a glass of beer over him. As you can imagine it was not the brightest thing to do. As Wilkinson moved toward him the drunk then threw the glass at him. Wilkinson threw up his arm and deflected the glass which unfortunately then stuck Henderson on the ear and resulted in a cut which later needed two stitches to staunch the bleeding.

It really was a disgraceful situation and one that prompted Corbett to write that the tourists should make the decision never to play in Mackay again. The two managers growing ever more conscious of the controversy that seemed to be following the players and the tour declined to comment and Henderson did not press charges. In truth the managers needed to have defended the players with a little more vigour, after all they had done nothing wrong. By saying nothing it simply gave rise to the view there was no smoke without fire. All of the feelgood factor from the win over Queensland was undone by the managers lack of action in defending the players. The tourists were glad to leave Mackay and head out up to Cairns to meet the Central Queensland side. The troubles in Mackay really were the last thing the tourists needed at that time.

It was just one more controversy in a long line of set backs they had faced since arriving down under. Poor and tired performances, a failure to 'gel' as a team, no matter which thirteen took to the field was problematical. Three loses and a draw and according to the media humiliation in the first Test. The constant sniping in the press at Greenall in particular and the real or imaginary rough or dirty play generally from the team. The banning of players from giving radio interviews and a lack of defence of the players by the managers in the press had further set them back. The uproar caused by the hiring of an Australian coach for the players both in Australia and at home causing Rawson to lose his place on the Management Committee had not helped. It was all proving very disruptive to player morale.

Now when they had put together two wins in Queensland and one against a very strong Queensland team to get the tour back on track they had the problems in Mackay. There was a growing belief in the press that the tourists were in disciplined when on the field, their play bordering on the illegal or even dirty. There was a big danger that the players, not all it must be said were getting away from the control of the two managers. If the tourists though things could only get better they were in for a rude awakening, a very rude awakening.

The game in Cairns while won with ease 39-18 produced more problems for the tourists. The team had been forced into some strange selections no more so than hooker Tommy Harris on the wing with Turnbull on the other. Turnbull who had been suffering from a leg injury since his arrival was again forced off when the muscles at the back of the thigh were torn thus keeping him out for at least another six weeks. Worse was to follow when Harris suffered a chipped ankle bone requiring his foot to be put in plaster and it was feared he was out for the rest of the Australian leg of the tour.

The visitors now only had one recognised hooker and two wingmen in Boston and O'Grady. When questioned the managers stated they would not be requesting additional players be flown out to join the tour. Henderson the prop was to be conscripted in as a make shift hooker for the rest of the tour. The tourists were now preparing to play North Queensland up in Townsville the game scheduled for the coming Sunday. The game was won once again going away by 30 – 11. The high light for the crowd was that both wingmen Boston and O'Grady scored four tries each.

For the managers at last they had some good news which they were quick to relay home, the tour receipts up to date were around £55,000. With the exception of the game played up in Townsville every other game had produced a record crowd. The managers were delighted that at least the financial side of things was turning out to be successful. The players now travelled to Rockhampton and the managers revealed that for the game against Central Queensland on the Tuesday again under flood lights they would play two forwards on the wings. Briggs would operate on one and Silcock on the other, for the latter that was no problem as he had in the past turned out for Wigan on the wing. It was to be something of a new experience for Briggs.

Given that the second Test was fast approaching the party was split and the ten players not required for the game at Rockhampton returned to Brisbane along with the manager Tom Hesketh. On that Tuesday evening once more controversy would rear its ugly head. Before that Rawson had another problem on his plate. At that time the two countries Australia and England had a transfer embargo in place. For a number of weeks the talk from the hosts had been of a plan for this embargo to be lifted when the Australian Board met on the 1st July. The hope being that the council in England would support such a proposal.

That being the case quite a number of Aussie clubs were quietly putting out 'feelers' toward some of the tourists to remain down under and play for clubs in Sydney or Brisbane. The players that had attracted particular attention were, Lewis Jones, Tommy Harris, Phil Jackson and Jim Bowden the prop. Other players were also said to be in the mix. Rawson and Hesketh faced the very real prospect of arriving in Australia with twenty-six players and arriving home with only twenty or even less.

On the Tuesday evening sadly, the old troubles returned for the tourists with poor play and more importantly rough play. Bill Corbett best summed up the match in his opening paragraph in the Telegraph the following day:-

'In the Rugby League "battle of Rockhampton" last night one of the touch judges saw his brother badly injured. It was one of the most chaotic matches I have ever seen."

One of the home team Tynan suffered a suspected fracture to one of the vertebrae in his neck and his brother had to continue running the touch line not knowing just how serious was the injury his brother had suffered.

Both sides blamed the other for the disgraceful scenes but in truth while both were equally as guilty, once again it was an inexperienced local referee that should shoulder the greater part of the blame. The first half was littered with players making second tackles and the English crashing into tackles with three or four men. It was a case of 'footbrawl' during the first forty minutes. John Henderson had to be patched up when the two stitches in his ear inserted up at Mackay were ripped out.

Brawls and fist fights erupted at regular intervals, on a couple of occasions Jack Cunliffe had to run in and break up such incidents. The Englishmen said after the game that the Queenslanders were 'lunatics'. Cunliffe was hit after passing the ball and was off the field for a time with concussion, the full back Cahill was hit well after he had kicked the ball. The Queensland player

Perrin suffered a similar fate in a chaotic first half. By the end of the match both teams were down to eleven men due to injuries. Duggie Greenall took exception at the number of times he was subjected to a late tackle and sought his own justice. On occasions he went in with stiff arm tackles which thankfully skimmed over the players heads.

During all of the mayhem the referee saw nothing that merited a player being sent from the field. Yet on many occasions one touch judge would be on the field to report an incident and the other touch judge would also be on for a different incident. The players did shake hands as the left the field with the tourists winning the game 21-12 but the press reports were all of yet another brawling game involving the visitors. It was just not what either manager wanted and Rawson tried desperately to play down the match to reporters. Once again instead of defending his players Rawson sought to make light of events that had occurred on the field.

It was not an ideal preparation for the vital second Test to be played in just three days time. The tourists had faced seven games in sixteen days and had just three days to prepare for the Test. Both Cunliffe and Cahill had been hospitalised following the Rockhampton game so would be out of contention for Saturday. Certainly, the Australian Board had lost patience with the growing controversy that seemed to follow most matches and declared that all future matches involving international teams would be refereed by the best officials available. They finally accepted the fact that inexperienced local officials were not up to the task. Unfortunately, as we shall see not all of the local authorities complied with this request with dire consequences.

While many were still tipping a home victory in the Test if not by the margin of the first, Corbett was of a different view. He felt the English were far stronger now than they had been in the Sydney Test. He was suggesting that victory would depend on Valentine, O'Grady and Helme getting through the game unscathed. All three were reportedly carrying injuries into this vital game but Corbett felt the Test was actually too close to call. One thing was sure, there were great match ups right across the park and the crowd was in for a treat.

On the Saturday at 2.45p.m. when the players took to the field a crowd of over 46,000 gave both teams a rousing reception. The teams for the Test were:-

AUSTRALIA:-
Churchill, Pidding, Hazzard, Watson, Carlson, Sullivan, Holman, Bull, Kearney, Hall, Provan, O'Shea, Crocker.

ENGLAND:-
Jones, Boston, Jackson, Ashcroft, O'Grady, Williams, Helme, Prescott, McKinney, Bowden, Pawsey, Silcock, Valentine.

The tourists had selected Williams the tour captain over Price to occupy the number six shirt and Pawsey had come into the second row allowing Valentine to come in at loose forward in place of Traill. If we are to believe the newspapers of the day then the skipper insisted on playing in the Test match and the managers succumbed to his demands. Given all the pressure the tourists faced it would be true to say they turned on a performance typical of other touring teams, dominating from first to last in a game that was end to end and thrilled those in attendance. It could also be that the rain that had made the pitch heavy and the ball slippery aiding the visitors more than the home side.

When the players walked on the pitch the Aussies were carrying toy kangaroos under their arms. The English not to be out done carried toy lions. With all the introductions over the match kicked off in light rain and the game turned the record book on its head yet again. If the Sydney Test had resulted in records the second Test out did them. The game was only a few minutes old when Pidding was penalised and Jones stepped up to give his team a 2-0 lead.

It was the visitors that were doing all the attacking contrary to expectations. Valentine combining with Prescott and Silcock to free Boston. With the cover closing in he cleverly kicked in field and it was Watson who was called on to save the situation. A little later Holman and Bowden got into a bit of a scuffle with punches thrown. Darcy Lawler the referee was quick and decisive and it was made clear to the players he was in charge not them. Then much against the run of play it was the home side that took the lead with a sensational try from Carlson.

It was O'Shea who broke through on his own twenty-five and quickly passed out to Carlson who sped past O'Grady and shot down the touch line. He cleverly chip kicked ahead regathered and touched down for a try by the posts. With Pidding converting the home side had the lead 5-2. The score had the effect of spurring on the visitors to greater efforts and they were to retake the lead a few minutes later. From a ruck thirty-five yards from the Australian line O'Grady took the ball and having made the break passed out to the supporting Pawsey. Pawsey powered out of Churchill's tackle and sprinted the last fifteen yards to the line for a try that Jones converted. The visitors were back in front 7-5.

It was now end to end stuff but it was the English who were continuing to dominate proceedings. The Aussie prop Hall could have given his side the lead but dropped the slippery ball over the try line. Then a little magic from Jackson got him a little room and he was able to free up Boston. Boston from five yards inside his own half straightened up the movement and when faced by Churchill side stepped and beat him with ease to score under the posts. With Jones converting the score went out to 12-5. There was no doubt the wet conditions and heavy ground were being made use of better by the Englishmen and at times they totally outplayed the home side.

The home side rallied and following clever work by Pidding Provan crashed over for a try which the former converted to close the score to 12-10. Jones was to extend the lead following a penalty in front of the posts to make it 14-10. With half time fast approaching it was the skipper Williams who managed to work an opening for himself and crossed for a try from close range. Once again, the reliable Jones added the two and at 19-10 were looking comfortable.

They could have been even more comfortable when a minute or so later Williams again was involved. His pass sent Ashcroft racing clear and he chipped the ball forward out to the wing. Boston swooped onto the ball and fell on it over the try line. To the amazement of the players Referee Lawler ruled a knock on and waved away the English protests. So, it was that the half time break saw the score unchanged. For the first time on the tour in a big match the visitors had not suffered a loss of concentration as the half was coming to an end and let the opposition back into the game.

The second half began as the first had ended with both sides attacking, first the green and gold threatened to score then the red, white and blue. In the forwards it was the proverbial arm wrestle but gradually the Englishmen began once more to get the upper hand once more. As is ever the case in such situations it was the under pressure Aussies who were to score first when Ashcroft made a mess of a high kick over his own try line. Hall dropped on the ball over the line for an unconverted try making the score 19-13.

Ashcroft quickly made amends for his error, getting the ball he created space outside the ruck and passed to Jackson. Jackson sold an outrageous dummy which sent two Aussie defenders the wrong way, when faced with the full back Churchill he passed out to Boston. With his speed there was no chance whatsoever that any one would lay a hand on the wingman and he crossed in the corner. It was Jones who then stepped up and from the touch line kicked a magnificent conversion and the score went out to 24-13.

They often say that games turn on a single event and perhaps that happened in this Test match. Holman and Boston got into a bit of an argument and referee Lawler called them out and read the riot act to the pair. Just a few minutes later Boston beat half a dozen defenders before passing out to Helme. Helme quickly passed on to the skipper Williams who cleverly passed back in field to Jones. Jones was then tackled by an Aussie who grabbed him by the left leg. Somehow Jones worked himself into a position that he dropped a goal with his right foot from fully thirty-five yards out while still being held by his left leg. It was a magnificent drop goal and the two points seemed to knock a lot of the stuffing out of the home side and at 26-13 they saw the Test slipping away from them.

The crowd when it sunk in what Jones had done cheered him to a man as he walked back to prepare for the kick-off. The Englishmen were now taking control and when Helme put Ashcroft into space the centre proceeded to beat three defenders and sent out a peach of a pass to his centre partner Jackson who crossed for yet another try. With Jones once more adding a conversion the score went out to 31-13. As if to rub salt in the wounds it was Jones who once more this time with time to spare slotted over yet another drop goal to add two more to the score board.

With the wind at their back the Englishmen through Jones were gaining a great deal of ground by kicking the ball down field. From one such kick Churchill in attempting to return the ball kicked it on the full into touch. From the scrum on the Aussie twenty-five yard line McKinney hooked the ball back and Helme completely bamboozled the defence and sliced through for another try, inevitably Jones added the extras and at 38-13 the game was effectively over. With their foot off the gas they allowed the home side to score two tries in the closing stages to make the final score 38-21.

The win by the Englishmen had been as comprehensive as the Aussies in the first Test and for the first time the visitors had played like a touring team should. They controlled every aspect of the game from first to last. As Bill Corbett wrote 'The Australians were never in the Hunt.' Lewis Jones kicked a record ten goals during the match to better Pidding's eight in the first Test. From being no hopers eighty minutes ago they were now looked on as favourites to win the third Test and with it the Ashes. One factor that contributed greatly to the win was the performance of the skipper Williams at stand-off. His speed over the heavy ground continually troubled the home defenders and the Aussie forwards could not lay a hand on him at times.

Inevitably the hoary old chestnut raised its head and folks questioned whether or not the Australians wanted to win the Test. After all, now all rested on the third and final Test and that was now a sell out following the tourist's performance. The answer to that question is that if they were not trying then it cost a number of them their place in the next Test and along with it a £30 match fee.

They had little time to celebrate the great win as the following day, the Sunday, they were in Toowoomba to meet the local side. The game was the last of the Queensland leg of the tour and a record 13,000 plus crowd turned out to see England win by 25-14. The tourists had gone through the Queensland leg of the tour undefeated and were feeling full of confidence. They were after all only the third tour party to do so as they emulated the 1914 and 1936 tourists. The problem was that when everything seems to be going well you just know that something is going to happen to upset the apple cart. When the tourists arrived back in Sydney the apple cart got well and truly upset!

CHAPTER SIX

The next game for the tourists was to be in Grafton in New South Wales where they were to meet the Far North side. In an effort to rest players once again seemingly strange selections were made. Silcock was again selected to play on the wing and prop Wilkinson selected to play in the hooking role. The game was not expected to trouble the visitors and so it turned out with an easy 44-12 win. Sadly, there were highs and lows for the tourists during the eighty minutes.

The game was marred by a mass brawl in the first half when Boston was tackled near the touch line and the Englishmen took exception to the tackle. Once again it was a case of a referee not really experienced enough to handle such a high-profile game. That was the low spot the high spot was also provided by Boston who turned on an exhibition of wing play of the highest quality. He crossed for six tries and in doing so showed his full repertoire of skills. His speed, side step, swerve and power were displayed in the tries he crossed the whitewash to score. The managers however were again on the back foot with the press in trying to defend their players against the allegations of dirty play. Once more they tried to play down the situation rather than defend the actions of the Englishmen.

With the tourists now back in Sydney the emphasis was on getting the Test players fit and free from injury for the up coming third and final Test. Before that they were to face a New South Wales side that was unbeaten during the season having defeated England once and Queensland three times. A provisional seventeen was named for the game on Saturday with the managers keeping the final selection close to their chests. What took place on that Saturday afternoon was to create history for the game, sadly for all the wrong reasons.

The afternoon of the game saw a persistent heavy rain fall and the ground was very heavy when the two teams took to the field. As they did so the rain came down even heavier quickly turning the pitch into a quagmire. The New South Wales officials along with the players were very angry as they felt the tourists were not taking the game seriously. The reason for that was simply due to the team that had been selected. When the tourists took to the field much to the annoyance of the 23,000 plus supporters only three Test players were on the field and there were some very strange positional selections. The team that went into this game for England was:-

Gunney, Wilkinson, Cunliffe, Greenall, Briggs, Price, Burnell, Harris, McKinney, Prescott, Henderson, Pawsey, Traill.

Looking at the line up you can see why the opposition would think the game was not being taken seriously. The problem was the managers had little other option as they could not risk those players wanted for the Test getting injured

When the game kicked of the rain seemed to come down even heavier and quickly turned the centre of the pitch into something resembling a lake. It was immediately obvious that the home side were superior and they began to take command even in the heavy going. With just three minutes gone the home side were across the try line and took a 5-0 lead. Then Pawsey put up a high kick which Cunliffe followed, caught and crossed for a try which was not converted.

Most of the play was restricted to the forwards as passing was almost impossible and from a mistake by Gunney the home side scored another try which they converted to lead 10-3. By now the centre of the field was becoming a skating rink with players slipping and sliding all over the place. In sliding players were crashing into the opposition players and tempers quickly began to fray. Yet another converted try gave the Aussies a 15-3 lead but the football was becoming somewhat of a farce. The score remained unchanged as the players left for the half time break.

Early in the second half with tempers becoming even more frayed and the tourists getting more frustrated with the officials the game became very rough. Duggie Greenall came in for particular attention and decided enough was enough. He hit Carlson with a high tackle as only Duggie could and that set the tone for the rest of the game. At a scrum Alf Burnell complained that he could not put the ball in the scrum as there was no tunnel. Finally, with the ball in Holman the New South Wales scrum half picked up and tried to run through. He was met by Burnell with a strong tackle that the referee Aub Oxford was not happy with. He called Burnell over and was promptly surrounded by complaining English players. Price the stand off must have said something to the referee and the touch judges who had also come onto the field for Oxford called him out and sent him from the field.

It seems that was the catalyst and the play became a series of running battles with the referee attempting to put out fires all over the park. There was some scoring, a penalty to the home side and a controversial try the referee awarded to Wilkinson. There was a great deal of slipping and sliding across the ground, pushing and shoving, punches thrown and boots flying. With just over twenty minutes of the game remaining the referee sensationally abandoned the game and walked off the pitch. For the first time in the history of the game a representative match was abandoned by the referee because of rough play.

Officials tried in vain to get the referee Oxford to continue but it is reported that he offered to give the whistle to one of them and told them to have a go if they liked. The actions of the referee were not only back page news but also front-page headlines as well. Bill Corbett wrote of the game on the front page of the Sun an article worth seeing in some detail:-

'Biggest sensation in NSW Rugby League occurred today when referee A. Oxford abandoned the England v NSW after a riot between players.
Oxford threw up his hands and walked off as players fought fiercely after fifteen minutes of play in the second half. A few minutes earlier Oxford had sent off English five eight Ray Price.
Every man in each team was involved when the brawl was at its height. The brawling occurred in the north-east corner of the ground when NSW led 17-6. Players stood toe to toe throwing punches. Others walked around looking for opponents at whom to fire punches. The amazing finish occurred when Alf Burnell English half back followed through and had a clash with NSW full back Clive Churchill.
Earlier there had been an episode in the English half involving Holman the NSW half back. As the referee intervened Englishmen gathered round him. Then

Oxford called out Price and sent him off. Immediately it was obvious there was to be some fierce football. Men were going in with tackles and jolting with elbows. Then the brawl broke out.

For some after time it went on even with the referee trying to quieten them. The referee took the right action. Both dressing rooms were barred after the game. As many players left the field they shook hands.

Tempers were too hot and conditions for the game were appalling. Rain fell practically throughout, handling was next to impossible and attempts at clever moves were ruined by the treacherous going. The centre of the area was a morass and players slid in all directions. This helped to cause frustration on both sides, and the blaze of temper.

When the brawling was at its top every man on both side was involved, with one general skirmish in the middle and several little private fights on the outskirts.

Mostly it had been a scrambling display of unspectacular football. The crowd was disappointing. This was due to both shocking weather and the fact that England had fielded a side contining only three second Test men and three forwards who were used as makeshift backs.

Officials will have to give players of England and Australia a sound lecture before they meet in the vital

Test next Saturday. Otherwise the brawling may occur again. It was a nasty jolt to the game, particularly international football.'

Photograph courtesy of Terry Williams at the NRL Museum

If the report were not bad enough for the game in general and the touring party in particular Corbett described a particularly serious and unpleasant incident involving one of the tourists that he witnessed.

'Several minutes after the players had left the field an ugly situation-unprecedented in the Members Stand-developed out side the English dressing room.

Englishman Price clad only in shirt and trousers climbed through a window onto the veranda of the dressing room and was promptly surrounded by around thirty supporters. In a few seconds heated words were being exchanged. English wingman Boston jumped through the window to support Price and it appeared as though blows would be struck. To jeers, hoots and yells of 'Get back to England!' England captain Dickie Williams came out onto the veranda grabbed both players by the arms and bundled them back into the dressing room.

Price gesticulating wildly, tried to force his way back onto the veranda but was eventually calmed by Williams and escorted back into the dressing room.'

It was an ugly incident and one that did not show the English in a good light. Following the game plain clothes policemen who were in the crowd were used to escort the referee Oxford from the ground. The problem was a simple one at first glance but in truth the problem was far more complicated. The match had been broadcast live by a number of radio stations. As was to be expected the Aussie commentators were not exactly unbiased in describing events taking place on the pitch. Every incident was attributed to English misdeeds.

The other complication was that the actions at the match and the way the visitors spoke to the officials was alien to the home players, officials and fans. Aussie players generally did not talk back to match officials. Also, while brawls did occur in domestic games the trouble stayed on the field and did not stray over the touch line. The actions of the referee Oxford in actually walking off the field, while lauded by reporters simply added to the impression that a riot was taking place rather than a game of rugby league. The fact was that only one player was dismissed, Ray Price the English halfback. It was later revealed he had received his marching orders for abusive language to the touch judges.

There was one other event albeit off the field which went unreported at the time involving the manager, Hector Rawson. He was involved in a serious incident while he was attempting to park the car he was driving to the ground. A parking attendant was injured as a result of the incident, Rawson left the scene and the police were called to the scene. A week or so later Rawson would face the consequences of his actions.

Photograph courtesy of Terry Williams at the NRL Museum

The recriminations after the game were swift from the press and it seemed no one escaped blame for the ruckus. On the Monday the Australian Board called a special meeting to discuss the events and deal with the players involved. The referee Aub Oxford after the game cited just three more players, Ken Traill and Alf Burnell from England and Harry Wells from New South Wales. They along with Price were to be dealt with by the committee on that Monday evening.

The two managers were also placed in the position of having to defend their own actions with regard to the team selection. Great emphasis was placed on the fact that three forwards were occupying both wings and full back spots. The impression gained from this by the players and New South Wales officials was that their actions had belittled the game. Hesketh and Rawson stated that they had ten men injured and for the game they had only one back fit to play. That was Lewis Jones and as they pointed out he was needed for the Test match.

Interestingly we see once again the attitude of the managers when faced with controversy of this nature on the tour. They asked Charles Pawsey who was captain on that fateful Saturday to apologise to the Australian authorities. This he actually did very begrudgingly. What really rankled the players though was that no one from the New South Wales team that day was called upon to apologise to the Englishmen for their part in the mayhem.

At the meeting there were calls for the gate money to be donated to charity, that all players be fined £10 or have their match fees rescinded entirely. None of which was done. The disciplinary action was that Price was suspended until 1st August, Traill, Burnell and Wells simply received a 'severe caution'. Such a decision would suggest that the action on the Saturday was not as bad as had been reported but certainly that was not the case, far from it. Certainly, it would seem the committee did not support the referee Oxford in his actions during and after the game.

On the Tuesday Corbett had obtained a copy of the referee's report to the authorities and printed it in the Sun. Oxford stated:-

'From the time I sent Price off I knew it was going to be impossible to restore order.
Practically from the outset England did not want to play football.
England used foul methods.
There was punching, stiff arm tackles, rabbit killers and boots were laid on. Others came in with their knees.
Bad language was used.
The Englishmen were saying they would 'get' certain players.
Three players in particular were named, Churchill, Holman and Pidding.

I say there was a definite object by some English players to put men out of action.

If I had allowed the match to continue I would have had to send off the players one by one.

Numerous players on each side were exchanging punches and were kicking and wrestling.

I did everything to get the Englishmen to play the game.

If I had to handle the match again I would take the same action.

I'd do the similarly in a Test match.

Linesman Nicholson said:-

The Englishmen used vile language.

Linesmen were subjected to abuse.

The Englishmen said get Holman, kick into Churchill. I saw Holman punched.

It is a pretty damning list of events but does prompt the question just why it took Oxford so long to take any serious action against the player on the pitch. The other point to note is that nowhere did Oxford aim criticism at the Australian players. In addition, while the Australian press and rugby authorities were having their say the troubles were causing the authorities back home to get involved. The Secretary Bill Fallowfield stated that they would await the report from the two managers before taking any action. The Chairman of Selectors Bob Anderton himself a former tour manager said that they could not judge from England but he was of the opinion that the referee had acted a little hastily in calling off the match before he had sent the teams off. He also quashed the notion that the tourists would be recalled and the third Test called off. He said that there was a great deal about the match they wanted to know before taking any action. The implication being that the two managers would be facing tough questioning on their return home.

There is no doubt the council back in Leeds was forced to take some action as the Yorkshire Post was scathing in its condemnation of events down under. The daily papers were also carrying articles about the abandoned game along with references to the incident in The Mackay Hotel when Henderson was hurt.

There is a very interesting aside with ramifications for the present day and that was the attitude to the Rugby League International Board. The board was condemned and blamed for the fiasco that occurred on the Saturday. It was stated that the English would propose it be scraped unless it :-

'is organised properly and efficiently shoulders the job for which it was created. That job is to obtain uniformity in interpretation of the laws in all countries.'

The French rugby league authority Secretary Antoine Blain who had attended a recent meeting in Brisbane of the International Board was scathing on his return to Paris.

'Australia and New Zealand will have to change their attitude and treat the international body as a permanently organised body controlling the game and not a conference held whenever and wherever it suits their convenience.'

Were it ever different with the present day NRL altering rules to suit themselves without reference to the International Board. The game played in the NRL is different from that played anywhere else in the world. At the time of writing the NRL is kicking up an almighty fuss over the Test match that is to be played in Denver between New Zealand and England. In truth the game has nothing to do with them but we see them treating the International Board in much the same way as they did during the tour.

It is strange to see that during the tour only two players were sent from the field, Briggs in the game at Mackay and now Price. In spite of this fact the tour seems to have been laden with rough games where referees have not had the best of games and play has got out of hand but no players were sent from the field. The press made a big issue of every discretion perceived on the field. In the case of Greenall it appears they were actively seeking out any wrong doing on his part real or imaginary.

All of this led to a feeling that the tourists were not really playing to the rules but rather trying as much as possible to play on the edge if not over the laws of the game. Within the game in Australia there was growing feeling that the two managers were losing control of a number of the players in the party. It must also be said that it was a feeling that was becoming ever stronger back in England as more and more stories of rough play were seeping back. The press also must share some of the blame as they were quick to condemn the visitors but slow to heap criticism on the home players.

Whatever the troubles were and they were many the tourists had not lost sight of the fact that they faced a third Test come the following Saturday and a Test which would decide the fate of the Ashes. The managers seem to have adopted the attitude of least said soonest mended and refused to comment further on the issue preferring the home authorities to deal with the situation. Once again, we see the managers failing to strongly come to the defence of the players in the press.

There was a little light relief for the tourists when news came through from home that the vice-captain Ashcroft had become a father for the second time or should that be a third time. On the Monday he received news that his wife had given birth to twin girls who were to be named Vivian and Elaine. In the midst of all the ongoing abandoned match saga the players proceeded to 'wet the babies heads'. They were able to let their hair down for a while and put the troubles behind them.

On the Wednesday the team to play the final Test was announced and the managers went with the same thirteen that had got the job done in the second Test up in Brisbane. They did get a scare during training at the Coogee Oval on that Wednesday when a stray dog ran onto the field, O'Grady tripped over it running at full speed and limped off as a result. Luckily it was not that serious and he was declared fit for the game on Saturday. It was also revealed that players in both camps had been told to cut out the rough stuff.

Immediately after the rough house on the Saturday calls had been made of the authorities to donate a sum of money from the gate to charity as we have seen. This call fell on deaf ears and a great many rank and file supporters were at best displeased and at worst disgusted by the action or lack of it from the board. It was a theme Bill Corbett revisited on the eve of the third Test in his column. He was of the opinion that their anaemic action would come back to haunt them later.

'Bad incidents are nine day wonders- a bit of soft soap and soon all is forgotten.
It isn't forgotten. Public wrath accumulates. Much the same point of view was held at Dunedin down in the South Island of New Zealand. League was looking

pretty good in this Rugby Union stronghold. Jim Sullivan's England team went there to play a South Island side in 1932. Both teams were guilty of intolerable punching, and League went out of existence in Dunedin for nigh on 22 years.'

The point he was making was a valid one namely that if supporters witness unacceptable behaviour on the pitch and little or no action is taken by the authorities then they will not return to watch international games again. In his column he went on to state that he had never seen so much dis-interest from supporters for the Test. As he wrote that had the all ticket game which was, a sell-out not been so then the gate would have been very low indeed. So, it was the whole fiasco turned out to be a nine-day wonder but only in the eyes of the authorities after all there was a Test match to play.

On the Saturday the Sydney Cricket Ground was packed as 67,577 turned up to watch the game almost two thousand more than had witnessed the first encounter.

Photograph courtesy of Terry Williams at the NRL Museum

The two teams for the game were:-

AUSTRALIA:-
Churchill, Carlson, Wells, Watson, Pidding, Banks, Holman, Davies, Kearney, Hall, Provan, O'Shea, Diversi

ENGLAND:-
Jones, Boston, Jackson, Ashcroft, O'Grady, Williams, Helme, Prescott, McKinney, Bowden, Pawsey, Silcock, Valentine.

If the supporters were expecting a repeat of the previous Saturday they were disappointed for rugby at its best was the order of the day. We shall never know if this was due to the stern warning issued to both teams or simply a desire to play the game as it should be played. When the game kicked off it was England that would dominate the opening quarter. They produced rugby that the home side could not match but as was ever the case on this tour the tourists failed to capitalise on their superiority.

Early on Boston got the ball and ran at his opposite number Pidding he side stepped him with ease and was only brought down a few yards short of the try line. A few minutes later Churchill put in a clearing cross field kick which only went as far as O'Grady on the half way line. With room to work in the wingman needed no second asking. He sped past Holman and as the cover defence raced across he passed inside to the centre Ashcroft who straightened up and scored in the corner for an unconverted try.

It was another mis-directed kick this time from Wells that proved the home sides undoing yet again. His kick went straight to the skipper Williams who returned the kick with interest. As the ball sailed past the full back Churchill, Williams raced through and beat every one to the ball to score. This time Jones did not miss and at 8-0 the Australians were seemingly out of it. Unfortunately try as they may the tourists could not add to the two long range scores. Prescott, O'Grady and Boston combined and almost got across the line only for the ball to go loose. The Australians were not helping themselves by kicking the ball high into the teeth of the wind so the ball was being blown back toward them.

From inside his own twenty-five yard area Valentine instead of kicking out threw a long pass to Williams. He fed O'Grady who ran around his opposite number and was only tackled by a last-ditch effort from the full back Churchill. Another chance went begging when Jones raced up into the three-quarter line and having got clear just as he was about to put Boston in the clear he slipped and the chance was lost. As is ever the case if chances are not taken the opposition come back and bite you. So, it proved when Churchill and Wells combined to put Watson in for a score by the posts. From being

seemingly out of contention the Aussies were now right
back in the game at 8-5.

Action from the Third Test. Carlson tackled.
Photograph courtesy of Terry Williams at the NRL Museum

Stung by this long range try the Englishmen came back strongly and Ashcroft and Jones put Boston away yet again and yet again a copy book tackle from Churchill saved a try. It was clearly the home side that were slowly beginning to get on top. From a ruck close to the England line Diversi who was making his debut gathered the ball, spun out of a would be tackle and crashed over for a try. Pidding stepped up, added the extras and the home side were in the lead 8-10. That was the score when the two sides went in for the half time break.

The writing was on the wall for the tourists as the second half began for with the wind at their back it was Australia that were attacking. Banks launched an attack and a reverse pass saw Wells race toward the line he was actually tackled by Bowden but Valentine coming in to assist in the tackle actually drove Bowden and Wells over the try line. Many in the crowd thought it was a double movement but Lawler rightly ruled a sliding try. The resulting goal took the score out to 8-15 and the Ashes were slipping away.

For a period of time the tourists had their backs to the wall as wave after wave of Australian attacks were launched at them. Much against the run of play it was the visitors that actually scored. It was Silcock who was the instigator getting free he saw Valentine out wide and his long pass put the Scot in at the corner. Jones kicking into a stiff breeze could not convert but at 11-15 the tourists were at least back in the hunt. It was that man Wells who was to strike yet again as he got clear and forced Boston to come in off his wing to tackle him. As he did so Wells passed to his wing Pidding who ran over unopposed and round under the posts. He converted his own try and took the score to 11-20.

With less than ten minutes left on the clock the situation looked hopeless for the tourists but Helme had other ideas. Picking up a ball he dummied first one and then another Aussie finally turning the ball inside to his skipper Williams. There was no stopping the little Welshman and he crossed for his second try. With Jones slotting over the two to take the score to 16-20 the last few minutes were to see the crowd roaring and cheering on the defence of Australia and the attack of the English.

In a desperate effort to save the Ashes the visitors were attacking at every opportunity and from anywhere on the field. The Aussies were equal to the task and held out and when another England attack broke down the bell sounded and the referee blew for full time. The Australians had regained the Ashes lost just two years earlier in England. The player shook hands and left the field to a tremendous reception from the crowd who had witnessed a thoroughly entertaining game of Test rugby.

There is no doubt that the win by the home side was due to the efforts of the pack who unlike in Brisbane stifled the English attack at crucial times. The tackling of the second rows and loose forward came in for particular praise as did the effort made by Harry Wells. In the end both sides scored four tries but it was the two extra goals from the boot of Pidding that made the difference. On such little things are games and Ashes won and lost. The tourists had played well but not consistently for the whole eighty minutes. That had been the story of the whole tour to date.

While the press tried to make an issue of the disputed sliding try by Wells the English skipper was having none of it. Williams told reporters that the visitors had been happy with the way Lawler had refereed the Tests and as he said, 'I was not in a position to see the disputed Harry Wells try. The referee seemed to be happy with it and that's an end to it. The Aussies played well and deserved the win.'

After the game Lewis Jones left the dressing rooms and either lost or had his wallet stolen. A search was organised but the wallet was not recovered. It was not the only thing lost that afternoon.

With the Ashes lost along with the Test the players could not relax and let their hair down for long as in a couple of days they were to catch an airplane bound for New

Zealand and that leg of the tour. Before they left the manager, Rawson was called to answer for his actions in the car park at the Cricket Ground on the day of the 'footbrawl' match against NSW the previous Saturday. Hector Rawson was up before the Magistrate on the Monday in the Traffic Court on the charge of negligent driving. The evidence given in court by the police sergeant relayed the tale.

It seems Rawson entered the car park opposite the Sydney Cricket Ground at around one o'clock on the Saturday only to be stopped by the car park attendant who demanded the two shillings parking fee. Rawson told him he intended parking over by a fence and was told he could not do so. Rawson told the attendant that he could park where ever he wanted. He promptly reversed and made a U-turn then drove at the attendant. The attendant was forced to leap clear and even then, was stuck by the car and bowled over injuring his arm, hand and leg. Rawson did not stop but drove away. When the police arrived, witnesses identified Rawson as the driver he claimed he did not know he had actually hit the parking attendant. He was charged with negligent driving and failing to stop after the accident.

He pleaded guilty to two charges and was slated in court by the Magistrate for failing to stop after knocking down the attendant. The Magistrate was of the opinion that:-

'This offence of negligent driving was a deliberate act in which the defendant did not consider the safety of the parking attendant. He continued to drive the vehicle toward him although the attendant was in front of him.'

The result was that Rawson was fined £22 and the image of the game was further damaged in the eyes of the public. It was also the final nail in the coffin for the Australian first leg of a tour that from day one had been dogged by troubles of one kind or another. The managers and players would have been glad to board the aircraft that would fly them over the Tasman Sea to Auckland and the New Zealand leg of the tour.

CHAPTER SEVEN

When the tourists arrived in Auckland they found that their reputation for rough and unsportsmanlike play had travelled across the Tasman Sea before them. The newspapers were fixed on the unsavoury aspects of the tour to date as they saw it. The New Zealand psychology with regard to such matters was far different to that of the Aussies. Even in 1954 any troubles on the field of play tended to be played down by the newspapers so for them to make a great play of games in Australia did not auger well for the visitors. Also, the Rugby Union authorities were quick to pounce on any league indiscretions. They seemed to have the ear of a sympathetic press and relished any rugby league indiscretion.

The first game of the tour was scheduled to be played on the Wednesday 21st July at Whangarei and the opposition was a Auckland Maori thirteen. The visitors must have felt they were back home as the rain came down, the field was a mud bath and a few minutes after kick-off the two teams could not be distinguished. One report of the game which the tourists won by a score of 14-4 stated that on more than one occasion the Englishmen were guilty of tackling their team mates rather that the opposition such was the level of mud coating both teams!

The match itself was uneventful apart from one rather unfortunate action by the two managers. The stand off Ray Price had been suspended following the NSW debacle in Sydney but took the field against the Maori. There was really no need for him to play in such a low-key game and the fact he did was discussed back in Sydney by the Australian Board of Control. Rawson was of the opinion that the rules allowed Price to play by reason of any suspension being only effectual in the country of the suspension. Price could not play in Australia but was free to play in New Zealand. Rawson had remembered a conference held in Blackpool back in 1952 when attempts had been made to make suspensions carry forward from country to country. That proposal had been defeated. So, Rawson was within his rights to play Price but his actions were seen as snubbing his nose to the Australian authorities. It only added to the growing belief the managers were unsympathetic to the Australian and New Zealand authorities.

While the tourists were in the Dominion Bill Corbett in his column on the Friday on the eve of the Test match in Auckland carried an interview with Dickie Williams the English skipper. The recriminations with regard to the quality of the tourists had been quite forceful in most of the newspapers and on the radio following the Test and Ashes defeat. Manny claiming the English were not of the standard of former tour parties. Others felt they were the weakest team ever to come down to Australia. In the column Williams sought to put the record straight.

'Why are we criticised the truth is the Australians have improved so much. I think the Australian teams that have won the Ashes were better all round than those who took the Ashes from England in 1950. I think also in most positions the 1954 Test teams were superior to those of 1950. England took a long time to hit form this time because the players did not have a trip by ship to recover from their long season and develop understanding. Some had not even played against each other. Don't bash England Boost Australia.'

It was in all probability a pretty fair assessment of the situation. The Australians had played well in the Test matches. The standard of play generally across the country was higher than it had been in 1950 but the press did not want to see that. There was more profit in bashing the poms as they had throughout the tour.

Over in Auckland the visitors were preparing for the first Test that was to be played at Carlaw Park on the Saturday, 24th July. The weather thankfully seemed to have relented and when the teams took to the field the conditions were ideal for playing rugby. There were over 30,000 supporters there to cheer on both teams. Hopes were high that the New Zealanders could knock over the

Englishmen as from what they had read of the tour to date they were vulnerable. The home selectors rather that selecting the players on form went for so called 'name' players. The two teams were:-

NEW ZEALAND:-
White, Eastlake, McKay, Baxter, Edwards, Menzies, Haig, Johnson, Roff, McLennan, Bond, Mulcare, Atkinson.

ENGLAND:-
Jones, Boston, Jackson, Ashcroft, O'Grady, Price, Helme, Prescott, Harris, Wilkinson, Gunney, Pawsey, Valentine.

The managers had selected a very strong side, particularly in the backs. Once again for whatever reason the tour skipper Williams was overlooked in favour of Price. The kick-off went smoothly for the visitors who kicked to the host side. When the New Zealanders got the ball and launched an attack it looked like they would score. The skipper Haig threw a long pass to his back line which had it reached its intended target would have resulted in a try for the New Zealanders. Sadly, for him Jackson the centre was alert to the situation and intercepted the pass. He burst through the home line and handed on the Boston who needed no second chance and quickly sped away from the pursuers to score in the opening minutes of the game.

The full back Jones duly added the extra two and the visitors were not finished. Just a couple of minutes later the other wingman O'Grady burst through the middle and once clear veered out to his opposite wing. There he found the ever-alert Boston who crossed yet again to take the lead out to 8-0. The same wingman would cross for a third try before the home side managed to tighten up the defence a little but at half time the score line read 13-2 to the tourists and in truth the home side had never been in the hunt.

Ashcroft was in sparkling form and Boston and O'Grady were not far behind and they continually cut the home defence to pieces. Pawsey and Valentine were the pick of the forwards and constantly secured good ball for the half backs. If the New Zealanders were poor in the first half they were woeful in the second half much to the disgust of the home supporters. Half way through the second forty minutes the supporters began walking out of the ground in droves. Boston crossed for his forth try, with Ashcroft bagging two and the hooker Tommy Harris chipping in with one. Jones could only manage three goals but the tourists left the pitch winners by 27-7. The score line in many ways flattered the home team as they had never looked like getting close to Ashcroft and his men.

With the Test match won the tourists travelled down to Wellington to meet the local side in a game on the Tuesday. It was an encounter that was not due to trouble the visitors and so it proved. O'Grady was in top form once more and crossed for five tries. Boston not to be left out went over three times as did Greenall. With McKinney bagging two, Cunliffe and Williams one each eight of which Jones added the extras too the score line ran out at 61-18.

It was an ideal preparation for the second Test that was to be played on South Island at Greymouth on the coming Saturday. The only problem, well two actually, was the rule interpretation by the local referee that caused tempers to become frayed. Hence the second problem that of accusations of rough play at best or dirty play by the visitors. In truth no one had seen tackling of the style that Duggie Greenall introduced to the players and the home supporters.

As the players travelled down to Greymouth news broke in the Sydney press that there was a proposal by the Australian Board of Control to play three Test matches against New Zealand in America. The plan was to play games on 24, 25 and 27th November on the way home from the first ever World Cup competition to be hosted by France. As was ever the case the plan never materialised and once again an opportunity to establish the game in the USA was lost.

The home selectors seemed to have learned the lesson from the first encounter up in Auckland and made five changes to the team that was to take on the Englishmen. The tourists made just three with Ashcroft carrying an injury Greenall replaced him. The skipper Williams reclaimed the stand-off spot and Briggs came into the second row in place of Pawsey. The two teams were:-

NEW ZEALAND:-

White, Edwards, Ackland, Baxter, Bakalich, Sorenson, Haig, Johnson, Blanchard, McLennan, Butterfield, Mulcare, Atkinson.

ENGLAND:-

Jones, Boston, Jackson, Greenall, O;Grady, Williams, Helme, Prescott, Harris, Wilkinson, Gunney, Briggs, Valentine.

The Crowd at Wingham Park on a perfect afternoon was just 4,240 but believe it or not it was a record for a West Coast match up to that time. One asks the question why play such an important match in such an out of the way venue? When the match kicked off it followed the beginning of the first encounter. Jones slotted over a penalty to give his side an early lead. That was increased when O'Grady crossed and Jones again added the extras. All the home side had to offer was a penalty of their own to make it 7-2. Another penalty closed the score to 7-4.

The visitors were on the wrong end of an increasing penalty count and tempers were once again fraying as the game was becoming a stop start affair. Still when Wilkinson crossed and Jones again obliged the score stood at 12-4. White the fullback was beginning to make England pay for the penalties and slotted two over to close the gap to 12-8. The play was becoming increasingly rough and in an attempt to control the situation the referee called both skippers together and read them the riot act. He was not going to have a repeat of the NSW debacle.

As the second half began it was the home side much to the delight of the small but enthusiastic crowd that scored first when Butterfield crossed for a try and White added his fifth goal. With the score now at 12-13 the visitors were awarded a penalty and Jones gave the lead back to his team. As play got rougher the tourists instead of sticking to playing rugby seemed intent on playing the man and the rucks saw punches thrown in profusion. The New Zealand forwards were now beginning to get the upper hand and Mulcare crossed for another try which once again was converted and the score read 14-18.

With the game coming to a close and the tourists throwing everything they had at the home side the referee stepped in once again and awarded a penalty to the home side. The tourists immediately protested the decision and mobbed the referee. It took the cool head of

Williams to calm the situation and lead his men away. White for the seventh time slotted over the goal to make the score 14-20 and the home side had scored a most unlikely victory to level the series. Not for the first time on the tour the Englishmen had let the odd decisions of the referee rattle them, stop playing the rugby they were capable of and resorting to retribution. It had the inevitable result yet again.

The tourists remained on South Island for the next mid-week game this time travelling over to Dunedin to meet South Island. The result was another easy win for the visitors 32-11. It was then on to Christchurch to play a match against Canterbury and a win by 60-14. The only notable thing about the game which was played in very heavy conditions is that Boston again crossed for four tries. Also, remarkably given the conditions Jones stepped up and kicked twelve goals.

The players then travelled back to New Plymouth up in North Island and on the Monday had yet another easy win defeating a North Island side 42-7. Lewis Jones seems to have continued his good form for not only did he score a try but also kicked another nine goals. The following Wednesday the tourists were in action once again this time playing South Auckland in Hamilton and again coming out on top 26-14.

The tourists while winning on the field were not winning off it. The belief was growing that when the going got a bit rough it was the tourists who were the instigators. Referees were constantly issuing cautions for rough play or for players disputing their decisions. It is difficult to state if the visitors were solely to blame as the newspaper reports are sketchy to say the least. One thing was certain the tour was leaving a nasty taste in the mouth for the New Zealand authorities, pressmen and supporters. It was in this atmosphere that the decisive third and final Test loomed back in Auckland at Carlaw Park.

The home side as you would expect having come out on top in the second Test selected the same team but were forced into one change when the wingman Bakalich was unfit and he was replaced by Austin who came in at centre with Baxter moving out to the wing. For the tourists Greenall made way for Ashcroft and the half backs, skipper Williams and Helme were replaced by Price and Burnell. In the pack Harris the hooker lost out to McKinney with Wilkinson suffering a similar fate replaced by Bowden. Briggs was replaced by Pawsey and Valentine by Traill. It seems that the managers had selected a pack of 'mud runners' once they discovered the state of the pitch. The two teams for the final Test were:-

NEW ZEALAND:-

White, Edwards, Ackland, Austin, Baxter, Sorenson, Haig, Johnson, Blanchard, McLennan, Butterfield, Mincare, Atkinson.

ENGLAND:-

Jones, Boston, Jackson, Ashcroft, O'Grady, Price, Burnell, Prescott, McKinney, Bowden, Gunney, Pawsey, Traill.

On the day of the game the rain which seemed to have been around for days had made the pitch a quagmire even before the players stood on it. Any chance of open football was highly unlikely and it was going to be an arm wrestle between the two packs. Given the tourist's record in such circumstances the referee was going to have his hands full. Sadly, that proved to be the case and the 6,186 brave and hardy souls who paid to watch the encounter certainly made their feelings known.

When the game kicked off the play was scrappy and the backs on either side saw little if any of the ball. On the odd occasion that football did break out it was the tourists who profited. First O'Grady crossed and then Price with Jones adding one conversion. In reply the home side managed three penalty goals from the numerous times the referee was forced to penalise the visitors. There were numerous pitched battles in the rucks which had the crowd hooting their derision at the Englishmen. Jones then on the one occasion he had the opportunity managed to kick a penalty to make the half time score 10-6.

The second half was dour to say the least the only score throughout the forty minutes being another Jones penalty. As the whistle went for full time the Englishmen were victorious and the Test series won. The constant battling and fighting that occurred in the second half certainly incensed the crowd who almost to a man remained in order to boo the visitors from the field. The manner of the win had displeased all except the visitors. Once again, we see a game that was filled with foul play and yet not for the first time the referee saw nothing that warranted sending a player from the field. Certainly, the home authorities were less than happy with the way the tourists played the game and expressed their anger to the two managers.

Sadly worse, far worse was to come for with the series over the authorities had arranged one last game this against Auckland. What transpired that afternoon just summed up what had been simmering under the surface during the time the players had been in New Zealand. The game was played at Carlaw Park once again and the pitch was a mud bath due to constant rain. Given it was to be the last game of the New Zealand leg over 9,000 braved the elements on the afternoon. What they saw perhaps shocked them it certainly upset the host authorities.

It was far and away the roughest and dirtiest game of the short tour which was not helped by both the conditions and the referee. As had been the case throughout the whole tour when the score had been close, the tourists seem to lose their temper at perceived injustices from the officials. That being the case they would proceed to seek retribution with both boot and fist. The game against Auckland was no exception as the brief report in the Sydney Morning Herald the day after the game showed.

'Auckland beat the English Rugby League team 5-4 today in the roughest game of the New Zealand tour. Frequent outbursts of fighting punctuated play, and eight or nine players joined in a brawl in the last few minutes. England players Nat Silcock and John Wilkinson were sent off the field for rough play. It was the Englishmen's last match in New Zealand, they return to Australia tomorrow. Auckland fullback Des White was taken to hospital after a hard tackle by the English centre Greenall. The game was played in heavy mud before a crowd of 9,000. All scoring was in the first half when Auckland got a try by Roff and a penalty goal by Grey, and Lewis Jones kicked two penalties for England. Auckland tired

badly towards the end but had enough in reserve to hold England. Nineteen penalties were awarded against England and six against Auckland. Auckland's forwards were superior to England's but England's backs handled better in passing movements when the opportunity occurred.'

While the report of the game is brief for the reporter to make mention of rough play as he did then the action on the field must have been far worse that reported. It seems that Silcock got involved in a skirmish just before half time and got his marching order from the referee. Early in the second half following yet another flair up Wilkinson made the long lonely walk. The troubles may well have been sparked very early in the game when the Auckland fullback White was stretchered off and taken to hospital following a Duggie Greenall tackle. It was a tackle that the authorities relayed in great detail to the authorities back in England at the end of the tour.

Certainly, the game was somewhat of a disaster for the authorities, it was so bad that the New Zealand authorities were so incensed that they determined to make a formal report and complain to the council back in England. The two England managers must have felt it was the NSW debacle all over once more. For them the tour of New Zealand could not end soon enough but they still had three games to oversee back in Australia before they returned home. They would also know they themselves would have hard questions to answer when the fronted the council.

Mind you at the farewell dinner in New Zealand the manager Rawson did not endear himself to his hosts. He reportedly said while addressing those present that the New Zealand Rugby League should get off the back of rugby union, depart from the forward type of play and develop a football entity of their own. It was not the most diplomatic thing to say at such a gathering. He then ruffled Kiwi feathers even more by saying:-

'Englishmen think New Zealand is only 'fooling' around with Rugby League, not going into it as earnestly and in the big way it should.'

If his first uttering was perhaps foolish what he followed it up with was down right tactless. If he expected the hosts to sit back and not respond in kind, he was sadly mistaken as he was to find out once he got back to Australia

CHAPTER EIGHT

The tourists left New Zealand on the Monday evening glad to avoid the newspaper publicity which surely followed the game. They arrived back in Sydney at 1.30am. On the Tuesday morning and settled back into their hotel. The troubles of the game against Auckland sadly followed them as the Sun printed a little piece about the state of the injured fullback, White. It was reported that he had suffered a rupture of the stomach following Greenall's tackle.

The article was supported by a photograph of Greenall who the press still looked upon as somewhat of a 'bogyman'. The article stated that White had been operated on during the Monday evening. The reporter continued with a little more of a dig writing, **'Greenall figured in several incidents in yesterday's match in which his team mates John Wilkinson and Nat Silcock were order off.'**

White was expected to be in hospital for a couple of weeks and would miss the World Cup in France in October. One wonders just what or how Greenall managed to do so much damage in a tackle.

The following day the Wednesday the tourists took on NSW once more and everyone hoped that there would be no fireworks this time. Well not everyone for around 20,000 turned up hoping for a repeat perhaps of the Aub Oxford debacle.

The game could not have started better for the English for very early in the proceedings Churchill cross kicked straight to Boston. He paused for a second and then set off pushing off one tackler and then another. As the cover came across he drew then in and passed inside to Valentine who scored without a hand being laid on him. The ever-reliable Jones added the extras and then rubbed salt in the wound a few minutes later with a penalty goal to make the score 7-0.

The NSW winger Carlson crossed for an unconverted try but Jones slotted over another penalty to take it out to 9-3. The tourists were slowly getting the upper hand and when Price sold an outrageous dummy that saw Ashcroft tackled without the ball, Price fed Jones who scored in the corner but could not convert. Holman cut the deficit scoring an unconverted try before disaster struck the tourists. Boston when tackled fell awkwardly and injured his left shoulder forcing him to leave the fray. In his absence Kite scored and when the conversion went over the score read 12-10. It stood at that as the players went in for the half time break.

Sadly, that was as good as it got for the visitors as their heavy schedule finally caught up with them and the hosts ran riot in the second half racking up a final score of 35 to the tourists 15. With Boston injured the total number of specialist wingmen fit to play now stood at nil. Castle and O'Grady were suffering from leg injuries and limping while Turnbull's injury had not responded to treatment and he had flown home early.

Prior to the game the two centres selected Greenall and Jackson pulled out. One can assume Jackson was injured but the implication with Greenall was that a change of heart by the managers was the result of his withdrawal. If the managers were attempting to minimise any bad publicity that seemed to follow Greenall all the tour then they need not have bothered. In the Morning Herald the following day right beside the match report was an article with the headline,

'BITTER ATTACK ON ENGLISH R.L. TEAM'

It was a pretty damning inditement of the tourists and is worth seeing in full.

'Auckland Rugby League Control Board members said tonight they would be 'just as happy' if Auckland was excluded from future visits to New Zealand by English League teams.
Frequent references were made at a Control Board meeting to the 'disgusting' play of the Englishmen at Auckland against New Zealand and Auckland.

The Chairman Mr. D.A. Wilkie said every game played in New Zealand quite a few of the tourists adopted rough-house tactics of a type calculated to maim a player.
The English team's record in Australia and New Zealand is no credit to the league game. Mr Wilkie said there was a lack of discipline among the players because of poor management. The action of six or eight undisciplined players disgusted their own team mates.'

It was an attack on both the players and the managers which demanded an immediate and equally forthright defence from Rawson and Hesketh the managers sadly it was not forthcoming. The tourists were down in Canberra to play a Southern Districts side and the Manager Rawson simply said he was amazed at the attack by New Zealand officials on the English players and managers. He stated:-

'No one passed any bad comments while we were in New Zealand and officials had every opportunity to do it.'

He went on to say that he was criticised by local officials when he asked them to postpone the game against Auckland on the Monday owing to the state of the pitch. It was a response that in no way supported the players in fact he made no mention of the claims of players trying to maim opponents. All in all it was a very weak response to a serious attack on the integrity of the players and himself.

The Auckland authorities at that meeting also suspended Silcock and Wilkinson for one month but as the players were now in Australia such a suspension would only come into effect if the two players were to return to New Zealand. It seemed that the managers were only concerned with playing the final games of the tour and getting on the plane home. Perhaps they thought that once they left Australia they would be leaving the problems behind also.

In fairness to Rawson in an interview with Bill Corbett in the Sun he did make a more spirited defence and also gives us an insight as to just what may well have been the cause of all the troubles.

'So called 'rucking mawls' in New Zealand Rugby League forward play would be referred to in England as 'indiscriminate kicking'.
We played the Test match in Auckland nearly throughout with twelve men. O'Grady was carried off.
In the first match of the tour John Henderson suffered a broken hand in the so called 'rucking

mawls' of forward play. Our captain Dick Williams was left in hospital after the Christchurch game. In the match against Auckland on the Monday first man off hurt was Valentine with an injured nose. First blow was struck by Auckland. Two of our players Wilkinson and Silcock were sent off and so should three Auckland players.'

The question is, was that defence strong enough or did we see typical English 'reserve' from Rawson yet again.

There was still further bad news for Rawson and Hesketh when it was revealed that the Rugby League authorities back home had cabled to their counterparts in both Australia and New Zealand. They were asking for reports on certain aspects of the tour and in particular the incidents of rough play that seemed to have punctuated the whole of the tour. It was seen as a further concern by the authorities in England about the way the tour was being run by the two managers and how certain players albeit a small number were behaving on the field.

The tourists were now more than ready for home but still had two more games to play. This also was to be in Australia rather than the USA as had been mooted earlier in the tour but it was difficult for the players to raise themselves for the encounters. They travelled down to Canberra to meet Southern Districts on the Saturday a game that went off without incident and saw the visitors win comfortably 66-21. That game over the players travelled up to Maitland to meet the Newcastle Coalfield side on the Monday. The game summed up all that had gone wrong on the tour and all the controversy that had dogged the visit.

If it was felt the last game before leaving would be more in the style of an exhibition game then nothing could be further from the truth. The game once again was the worst nightmare for the game in general and the players and managers in particular. It was a game that rivalled that against New South Wales which had seen the referee Aub Oxford abandon proceedings and walk off in terms of controversy. Before the game all had seemed to be going smooth enough.

The players were left in the hotel and the managers along with the skipper Dickie Williams attended a ceremony at St Pauls Church in Maitland. There they laid a wreath on a tablet in the church to the memory of the former England captain Robert Seddon. Seddon who had drowned in the Hunter River while leading the English rugby union tour in 1888 following a boating accident. It was a gesture that was much appreciated by the local rugby community of both codes. It has to be said that from that point on friendly relationships took a turn for the worse.

Given this was to be the last game of the tour a great many Australian League and Board officials were in attendance and what they saw horrified them. Two in particular Harry Flegg and John Quinlan had no love of the Englishmen and they were to report on the game to a special meeting of the Australian Board on the day after the match. When the game began it seemed that all would go off with no problems. Then the Greenall factor kicked in.

Greenall had been maligned all the tour both for his style of play and perceived illegal tackles on the Australians way back on the 1952 tour. With twenty minutes of the game gone and the visitors seemingly coasting at 10-3 the problems began. The referee Sneddon who was from the Manning River League stopped the game and called Greenall over. It is then alleged that he accused the player of having plaster on his forearm and using it when making his stiff-arm tackles on the opposition.

It was perhaps a complaint too far for Greenall who walked off the field pulling his jersey off as he left. The skipper Ashcroft and a couple of other players tried to stop him leaving the field but he left. He was met on the touchline by Hector Rawson and a fierce argument erupted between the two. Dickie Williams the tour skipper and Ken Traill intervened and seemed to calm the situation down. Greenall returned to the field and pulled up his sleeve as he approached the referee to show he was wearing nothing illegal.

It was revealed later that the Newcastle skipper Dave Parkinson had actually complained to the referee about the stiff-arm tackles Greenall was making and getting away with. Something must have been lost in translation hence Greenall's walk off but the Aussies had history with Duggie. In the second Test at Swinton he had knocked out the Aussie centre Hazzard with a stiff-arm tackle and when the players went to the dressing room to exchange jerseys Aussie players saw one of his arms strongly bandaged. The referee perhaps felt the same was happening that afternoon.

With Duggie back on the field the referee called all the tourists together along with the Newcastle skipper and tried to settle both sides down sadly he didn't. In fairness to the tourists they must have been heartily sick of the constant sniping at one of their own from all sides and sought their own retribution. In the rucks punches were thrown and boots flew with a greater frequency than was legal. In the last twenty minutes of the first half at least three brawls broke out. The referee was out of his depth and try as he may could do little to stop the mayhem.

The authorities in Newcastle had ignored the directive from the Australian Board with regard to the referee appointed to such a match and paid the price, sadly so did the game. There was not one player sent from the field in the hope that it would cause some sanity to return to the game. The touch judges were constantly running on the field to report incidents yet the referee was blind to the foul play. It was a case once again of an inexperienced official being given charge of a highly emotional game.

When the second half began many felt it was lucky that the game had not followed the path of the New South Wales encounter and been abandoned. Early on play was held up on a couple of occasions when the touch judge came on the field. From a scrum the packs erupted and punches were thrown and barely had that settled down when Valentine floored the opposing stand-off with a right hook to the jaw. While the Englishmen were losing their tempers', they were also losing the game as Newcastle had taken the lead.

Yet more brawls erupted and the referee still refused to send players for an early bath and the crowd was becoming more volatile. Then Pitman the home second row and Valentine 'squared up' and punches were thrown worse was to follow. Still the referee took no action. When Smeddon and Briggs had a punch up shortly afterwards it sparked yet another brawl amongst the forwards. The skipper Ashcroft tried to maintain some semblance of order and calm his players down but the referee had now totally lost control. His answer to the problems was to stop play for a while to let tempers cool but no player walked.

When the game ended the score was relatively unimportant but had seen the home side prevail 28-22. The recriminations began almost immediately but it seems only from the home authorities. Flegg and Quinlan went into overdrive as did the Board Secretary, Matthews. He claimed matters would be discussed on the following day and as requested a report would be prepared for the authorities back in England. Hector Rawson for his part when questioned by reports stated that Greenall had not walked from the field he had merely come to the touchline to complain about the referee's allegations.

The local reporter for the Newcastle Sun tells us that When Greenall returned to the field he got quite a bit of stick from the crowd for the rest of the game. Duggie however, was not one to take such actions lying down as the reporter explained:-

'The crowd irrespective of rights or wrongs, gave Greenall "the works". But he crushed them with a word. During one outburst, he turned, cupped his hands and shouted back "convicts!"'

That seemed to have quietened the watching crowd.

Then with all the mayhem going on around him regarding dirty play Rawson stated that he was to dispute the gate receipts the Newcastle authorities were claiming. The gate was around 11,000 and some £2,058 in the coffers of which 65% went to the tourists. It was a crass attitude to take but perhaps it was meant to deflect attention from the major issues that had dogged the tour all the way through. Certainly, he had consistently attempted to deflect criticism rather than challenge it all through the tour.

The final ignominy for the players at the end of this troublesome tour came following the last game. When the players came to get dressed after showering following the game they found that the metal lapel badges they had been collecting during the tour had been stolen. The badges of the Lions, Kiwis and Kangaroos had gone missing when the dressing room had been crowded when the players were getting changed. For the players it was a sad end to a sad tour.

On the Monday in the Sun Corbett pulled no punches and quite radically stated:-

'Officials of all Rugby League countries must take drastic steps to stop illegal violence for all time. Otherwise international football shouldn't be encouraged. It would be sound policy if international games were suspended for a period of years until

sanity returns to the game. Club football can prosper in England and Australia without international football. Both countries would be given a chance to settle down. Old grievances would be forgotten. Bitterness between English and Australian players started on the tour in 1952-53 of England. It smouldered in the meantime and broke out again on the present tour.'

They were very strong words and give a good idea of the seriousness of the situation a seriousness that seemed to by-pass the two managers and as we shall see the Australian Board. It was only as the tour was coming to its end that action was being taken in any sort of shape or form. It was a case of too little too late. Once again Hector Rawson seems not to have grasped the seriousness of the problems, if the interview he gave at the airport on the Tuesday morning just before the tourists boarded an aircraft bound for home was any indication.

He told reporters that he would make a report to the English League on **'incidents that had occurred during the Australia and New Zealand tour.'** His comments lead one to question what planet he was on given what had gone on during the tour. He continued and told the reporters present:-

'I think in every tour there have been a few incidents and misunderstandings. This may be due to the contrast in play in Tests and the play in other games. I don't know. One cannot be rough on his own. That is generally understood. There is the old saying there is two sides always in everything.'

Rawson then attempted to gloss over events that had transpired in Australia and New Zealand that caused such upheavals:-

'It has been an excellent tour financially and from every other angle. We have kept good faith throughout and made many friends. I am sure misunderstandings there has been in the past between England and Australia and between England and New Zealand have been entirely wiped out. Our own connection between Australia and England I consider is on a better footing than ever.'

One can only assume Rawson was playing 'a straight bat' as it were with his comments. The 'Battle of Rockhampton', the Mackay incident the abandoned game the problems in Newcastle. The claims of rough play in New Zealand in the third Test and the game against Auckland he seems to have forgotten about. Equally stupid was his claims of all being well, the Australian Board, New Zealand Board, Auckland Board all of them were writing a report to the council back home with regard to the conduct of certain players on the tour and the lack of strong management.

Mind you the previous evening at a farewell dinner held for the tourists neither the English or Australians made any mention in the speeches of the rough game in Maitland. Neither did they make any reference to all the other unpleasant events that had occurred on the tour. Tom Hesketh thanks the Aussies for the £65,000 cheque he had received from the Board. One point neither side could agree on was the decision to fly the players out to Australia.

The skipper in his remarks felt too much had been made of that and as he said by the time the Test matches came around the players had really settled down. Harry Flegg on the other hand for the Aussies was of the opinion the crowds had not seen the best of the tourists. He expressed the opinion that there would be no more flying trips after a long hard season from the English. Today little is made of the fact that players fly down to Australia back then it was a different story.

At the dinner each of the tourists were given a silver teapot as a memento of their trip. The players were a little more forthcoming than the manages had been when they spoke with the Herald reporter Tom Goodman. Many of them expressed the opinion that they were pleased to spend a little time in comradeship with the opposition and felt the tour had been a very unpleasant one. They were tired of football and soured by the **'long series of unsettling disturbances on the tour.'** Goodman expressed the view that it was the most unfortunate tour he had ever covered in spite of the record profit. All were agreed that something needed to be done in the future be it rule changes stricter refereeing by experienced officials and better discipline from the players.

On the three-day journey home both Rawson and Hesketh must have realised that once in front of council they would face difficult questions. What they now had to do was ensue they were both singing from the same hymn sheet when writing their report. They would point to the record receipts and attendances from the tour as a sign of their good handling of the tour but it would have been a troubled pair that touched down in England.

CHAPTER NINE

Back in Australia while the domestic game took over the media and the games authorities were eagerly awaiting just what the outcome of their own actions with regard to the events on the tour would bring. The Board was busy preparing a report on the rough and illegal play of the Englishmen. It was their intention to send the report over to the council in Leeds. Rawson and Hesketh for their part were busy also writing a comprehensive report of the tour. History shows that they were not in much of an hurry and were perhaps having second thoughts with regard to the strength their arguments should take as we shall see. On the 13th September the Rugby League Council meeting was held and at it they received the report of the two managers. As they did so council was still awaiting the Australian report on the tour!

It was Rawson who rose to his feet that day and read the report to council. The report ran to fourteen pages and covered a number of aspects of the tour. Rawson began by speaking of the game against New South Wales that had been abandoned. He claimed that it was this game in particular that had there after produced a situation were so called incidents were greatly magnified by all in the press. He went on to report on first the game up at Mackay.

It was the managers contention that two factors had contributed to the incidents during the game. The first was an incompetent referee and the second a very hard ground. It was revealed that at their request the fire brigade had been asked to watered the pitch. Local officials stated that had been done when in fact it had not. Then the referee had favoured the home team in standing off side and waved away criticism from the tourists. The referee had little control of matters in the second half and had sent Briggs from the field and cautioned Bowden. Strangely the report makes no reference to the incident at the Mackay Hotel in which Henderson cut his ear.

The report then detailed events at the so-called Battle of Rockhampton game. The report highlighted the fact that late tackles by the home side were not punished by the local referee. Rawson hinted that at the half time break the tourist forwards were keen to get at the opposition. They told him they had been repeatedly punched while packing down in the scrum. Rawson told the players to remain calm and keep their temper under control. He then visited the home dressing room and spoke with officials telling them to cut out the rough stuff.

In defence of the managers they did not try to hide the rough play but attempted to relate just why it had occurred. The notorious New South Wales game in their opinion saw rough stuff begin really in the 46th minute of the game and continued until the 55th minute when the referee left the field. In the 46th minute a touch judge had run onto the field to report an incident. Pawsey who was captaining the side along with Burnell and Price approached the referee as did a number of the Australians. Pawsey argued against the report from the touch judge and the culmination saw the referee dismissed Price the stand-off for bad language.

When the game restarted Bull had taken a swing at an English player and was cautioned by the referee who was then approached by Greenall who asked why the player had not been sent from the field. The real trouble had begun when Burnell had attempted to charge down a kick from Churchill the full back. Burnell slipped in the mud and in doing so slid into Churchill after he had kicked the ball knocked him to the ground. Pidding had then run in and punched Burnell and a melee ensued. Players from both sides started to fight a situation which lasted for around half a minute. When it stopped the referee walked off the field.

The crowd shouted their derision as the tourists left the field and a number of them made rude gestures to the supporters. The managers called all the tourists into the dressing room and gave them a thorough dressing down. Again, no mention was made of the Price incident when he left the dressing room to argue with supporters. The managers were of the opinion that the referee Oxford really had no idea of the seriousness of his action in leaving the field.

Once again strange as it may seem the report made no mention of the last game of the tour up in Newcastle. This game in the opinion of many was far worse that the abandoned state game and yet Rawson and Hesketh made no reference to it. Perhaps they took the stance 'let sleeping dogs lie'. They did address the issue of the Auckland match in New Zealand perhaps in anticipation that the authorities in that country had written to the council. The ground was in an atrocious state and that played a part in proceedings. Early on Valentine was laid out and forced from the field for a time. There were many incidents where the opposition with ball in hand played the man rather than the game. Late tackles were the order of the day. The manager felt the crucial issue in the game came when a scrum was forming and Jolley struck Wilkinson who retaliated. Jolley seemed to go berserk and ran around striking out at all in his way. The referee attempted to calm the situation but later Jolley and Wilkinson clashed again and the Englishman was sent from the field. Later Silcock was also dismissed but no home players were to receive such orders.

The report raised a number of issues the main one being the differing interpretation of the rules by Australian and New Zealand referees. The report also suggested that when selection of players for international matches selectors should consider his record and clean type of play. Both managers were very critical of the way in which Greenall had been demonised by the press even before his arrival. It was a persecution that had been maintained throughout the tour. They were of the opinion that the players had been very well behaved all through the tour.

The fact was that council had little other evidence to consider apart from the letters received from the New Zealand Authorities. They were still awaiting the report from the Australian Board. When it did arrive, it was very much a watered-down version to that expressed at the time by officials. They seemed to have been affected by the adverse press coverage the tour had received and the blame being apportioned to each side.

I think they simply wanted the whole matter to go away. They expressed the opinion that stricter consideration should be applied when appointing referees. That when players are sent from the field more severe punishment should be administered to those players. Finally, they felt greater care should be exercised in screening players selected to tour. In that at least, they were in agreement with the two English managers.

The report which was a single sheet of paper was really quite weak in its condemnation when compared to comments made at the time by Australian officials.

'We are of the opinion that grave incidents happened in matches played in Queensland and New South Wales. Some players who took part in them and were detrimental to the welfare of our Rugby League game. In several instances the refereeing was of a weak standard of which we feel some players took advantage of.'

With regard to the abandoned match which had caused them so much consternation at the time the simple stated:-

'The match, Great Britain versus New South Wales.... Was a disgrace to our code and the incidents unparalleled in the history of our game. This match is the only occasion when a Referee found it necessary to abandon a match of such importance and we have sent you a copy of our inquiry.'

The inquiry was not made public by the council but we can only assume it was couched in stronger terms than was the report. However, the Australian version of events as stated by the report shed little light on events unlike their counterparts across the Tasman Sea.

The New Zealand authorities were far more forthcoming when they wrote their report to the council. They expressed the opinion that a small number of players in the tour party were not up to the standard of sportsmanship and control expected of a touring team.

These few by their actions on the field made the whole party unpopular. The authorities then listed a number of objections.

Unnecessary brutality in making tackles.
Second tacklers heavily completing a tackle on an already held player.
Deliberate late tackles.
Interference of players chasing or following the ball.
Punching in the scrums.
Players instead of preventing clashes actually running in and adding to the melee (The offence Wilkinson and Silcock were dismissed for.)
Unnecessary provocation of players by forcing their head into the ground in the course of a tackle.
Unnecessary antagonism and quarrelsome attitude.

They actually cited the case of Greenall's tackle on White in the Auckland game when he had hit White in the stomach with both knees in the tackle. The result was that White suffered a rupture to the intestine near the stomach.

'We would draw to your council's attention that D.H. White an international player with an excellent reputation for clean play is now in the Auckland hospital dangerously ill having been the subject of a severe operation, the result of which is not yet fully known but it is realised that after such a severe operation the player's playing career is finished and it is doubtful whether he will ever enjoy thoroughly good health again. The tackle which caused this was made when White took the ball in a passing movement and D. Greenall jumped into him and brought both knees into White's abdomen. Subsequent surgical examination revealed that this had ruptured the intestine near the stomach.'

It has to be pointed out here in defence of Greenall that the referee did not take any action as he considered Greenall's tackle to be perfectly legal. The authorities were also critical of Rawson's attitude while in the country. Stating he had the unfortunate practice of conducting a controversy against New Zealand conditions and style of play through the newspapers.

What they found upsetting about this attitude was the fact that the newspapers were unfriendly toward the league game and took great delight in giving undue publicity to dissension within the League game as a whole. So, for a senior figure in the game to persist in making statements to the press that were both controversial and derogatory did nothing to help relations between the two authorities. In support of the report the New Zealand authorities also enclosed press cuttings and photographs for council to see. It was obvious that the council would need to address the issues raised formally by New Zealand and tacitly by the Australians and address them as soon as possible.

On other issues in the report Rawson gave there is a number of recommendations made by the managers. They felt there should be more games played on the tour and to accommodate this perhaps the party should consist of thirty-two players rather than the present twenty-six. They also advocated the appointment of a coach to accompany the players. While supporting the notion of travelling by air they recommended that tourist class was not suitable. They also felt that three Test matches in New Zealand were essential but they should be played in Auckland and Christchurch.

The managers did make one very interesting and far sighted recommendation at the conclusion of the report which sadly was not acted upon. The suggested the next tour should fly out via America with a view to playing two games in that country. Then they should fly to Honolulu where they believe a match could shape the interest of the locals. They actually named a former American Footballer who was keen on the game believing it to be better than American rugby. Steve Drakalich had informed them many in the Islands were splendid athletes. Rawson then informed members that he had two promoters who were interested and wanted to hear from him once he had reported back to authorities in England. Rawson stated that a boat trip from Hawaii to Auckland should be arranged and New Zealand visited first then onto Australia.

His reasoning was and still is very sound as in April and May there would be little or no competition from the Rugby Union authorities via their Ranfurly Shield competition. Sadly, this proposal never saw the light of day and it is only now that the NRL are proposing to play a game in Hawaii at the beginning of the 2019 season along with a game in America. It has only taken around sixty-five years for the game to get really serious about the game in America.

With the report completed there is no doubt a great deal of discussion ensued of which the public were not privy. The evidence suggests that certain players were condemned for their behaviour on the field and arrangements made to deal with them severely should they transgress in the domestic game at any future period. To suggest a blacklist was drawn up may well be too strong a term but for sure players were on notice. Also reading between the lines it appears that a record of disciplinary misdemeanours was going to be set up and that record referred to when selection came around for international matches and tours.

The council did write a report of the tour in response to the New Zealand authorities letter. In it council laid down plans to deal with future tours and internationals. It is rather sad that with the tour well and truly officially over and the players back with their respective clubs that the ramifications were still ongoing. They laid out proposals they intended to put before the International Board with regard to player behaviour on the field in regard to language and provocative behaviour. Most importantly they felt the two managers had endeavoured at all times to get the players to play the game in a proper spirit. Given they had not at that time received the Australian report there was little else they could do.

What we do see from the report produced by the council is that certain players whose behaviour directly led to the undesirable incidents on the tour were known to them. They also felt it important to look at ways of preventing such incidents occurring again. They also hinted that at times the managers would have liked to suspend a troublesome player to bring them in line. However due to the injury situation on the tour they were unable to do so. Finally, the report called upon all countries to pave the way for a better understanding within the game with regard to expected behaviour from players along with rule interpretation being consistent.

Down in Australia once details of the managers report and council's response was known the press went to town. Tom Goodman writing in the Herald did so under the headline:-

ENGLISH R.L. 'BLACK LIST'

In the article he claims that the managers had reported to council very strongly against certain players. He stated that **'A black list of this minority has been arranged-It would not be difficult to guess some of the names.'**

In actual fact what the council said in a press report was:-

With reference to the 1954 tour, the names of those players whose behaviour was the direct cause of undesirable incidents are known to the council.

That is a little different to a black list being established. However, they went on to say that those players would be made known to the selection committee and their chances of selection for future international teams would be prejudiced. It is still some pretty strong action against the still un-named players from the tour.

In the article Goodman made the point that it was obvious that the English would 'whitewash' the two managers which was a little unfair given the weakness of the Australian report when it finally did arrive:-

"England was bound to put the blame on 'both sides' that played in the unruly games in Australia.'

It is hard to see what else could have been said it does take two to tango they say.

The question is, was there really a black list of players, certainly some from that tour never were to wear the red white and blue jersey again. That is one explanation the other is that perhaps other players came through and took priority when it came to selection for international games and tours. Yet another explanation is the aging of players or loss of form leading to non-selection. The reader will need to make up his or her own mind on that whether or not a blacklist was ever drawn up by council.

There is a very interesting post script to this issue of a so called blacklist and it appears in the Sun on the 21st September soon after the players returned home. The article stated that Nat Silcock had been sent-off in the final minutes of the game against Keighley. It is what comes after that makes interesting reading:-

'Silcock is believed to be one of the recent tourists to Australia and New Zealand who was placed on the "black books" following the manager's report.'

This would indeed support the notion that certain players were, if not blacklisted, were looked at with less favourable eyes when international selection came around. The article went on to say that two other tourists Ken Traill and Charles Pawsey had been ordered off since their return and received a six-match suspension.

Those who suspect that there really was a blacklist as many down in Australia believed may well have found some support when the party for the first ever World Cup tournament was announced. In an article printed in the Sun on 1st October but written by a correspondent in England. It was revealed that only five players from the tour were in the squad. Some players were out injured, some withdrew due to the poor financial rewards on offer to go to France but the article stated:-

'Henderson, Bowden, Traill, Briggs, Harris, Burnall have been passed over some of them have been blacklisted in manager Rawson's tour report.'

That was patently not true as in the official report Rawson named no players. However, the discussions by council held in private may well have seen a list of names drawn up but we shall never know. For whatever reasons both Pawsey and Silcock did not give the selectors the satisfaction of passing them over as they withdrew themselves from selection. The reader must make up their own mind as to whether a player blacklist was drawn up by the council or not as stated earlier.

With regard to council's report on rough play and its recommendations one thing all were agreed on was that if a player was suspended then the suspension should be observed in all countries. Other recommendations they proposed were to be put to the International Board when it met in October during the forth coming World Cup competition in France. The outcome of those recommendations and the effects they were to have on the game are as they say, a matter for another day or should that be another book.

There was though one very interesting comment about this whole situation of rough play from the French Rugby League Secretary Antoine Blain. His comments were referred to by Corbett in his column on the 17th September. Blain's suggestion was not to see the light of day until very much later in our game:-

'What we need is proper action by a referee in calling an offender off-field to cool down. I think players would soon come round.'

It sounds to me very much like the present day 'sin-bin' that operates in the game.

What is really sad is that the tour with all its controversies saw a very important fact for the British game overlooked. When you look beyond the rough play and unsavoury incidents that occurred in Australia and New Zealand, what this tour did was to produce a really great number of young players who would go on to grace the game for many years. Two young wingmen in Boston and O'Grady, two great centres in Jones and Jackson. Three great second row forwards in Silcock, Gunney and Briggs. Jim Bowden came through as a good young prop forward as to did Jack Wilkinson. Also, a future tour captain whose courage would become the stuff of legends in the prop Alan Prescott. Other players bowed out of the international scene for what ever reasons as always happens after such tours.

With the benefit of hindsight one of the major failings of the tour was that the players never seemed to 'gel' and if they did they were not consistent in that. There is a saying that a Champion team will beat a team of champions and perhaps that is why the Ashes were lost on the tour. Would the team have 'gelled' any better had they travelled by sea that we shall never know. The tenth tour to Australia and New Zealand should have been lauded for the number of young players it brought to the fore in the game some becoming 'greats of the game'. Instead it became known as and still is considered the most controversial tour the Rugby League ever undertook. It was a sad inditement of the game and truly was the turbulent tour.

PLAYER PEN PICTURES

It should be noted that the pen pictures below were the work of the reporter of the Sun Newspaper in Sydney. They were written from information gleamed for official sources in England once the tour party was announced. Some are quite brief as the players were relatively unknown to the reporters down under.

DICK WILLIAMS (Hunslet)   Stand-Off
Age 33   Height 5ft 8ins   Weight 11st. 4lb.
Holds a B.Sc. Degree, works in civil engineering department of Leeds Corporation. Announced retirement this season when Leeds put him on the transfer list, but after Hunslet signed him for one season began training hard. Toured in 1950, playing in two Tests, and captained Britain in the 1951 Tests against New Zealand.

CHARLES PAWSEY (Leigh)   Second Row
Age 29   Height 6ft.   Weight 14st. 13lbs.
Wharf labourer. Second rower of the Doug Phillips (1946 tour) type, powerful, hard hitting, and with exceptional pace in open. Made international debut for England against Wales in September 1952, and before the end of that year had played in three Tests against the Kangaroos.

BRIAN BRIGGS (Huddersfield)   Second row
Age 21   Height 6ft.   Weight 14st.
Warehouseman. Recently bought from York. Was signed by York while still in the Army, and only played one full season with them. Briggs is ginger-haired, fast, and tireless second rower.

WILKINSON JACK (Halifax)   Prop forward
Age 24   Height 6ft.   Weight 14st. 8lbs.
Very strong and a wrestler in spare time. Is fast for his size. Played for England against Other Nationalities this season.

HARRIS TOM (Hull)   Hooker
Age 25   Height 5ft. 7in.   Weight 12st. 10lbs.
Engineering labourer. Played Rugby Union in Wales when signed by Hull in 1949 as deputy to Australian George Watt. Soon after he took over as No 1 hooker. Is the fastest hooker playing Rugby League in England.

McKINNEY TOM (Salford)   Hooker
Age 26   Height 5ft. 10ins.   Weight 14st. 7lbs.
One of few Irishmen playing Rugby League. Has represented Britain in three Tests including two against 1952 Kangaroos. Regarded as the best hooker since Joe Egan, but habit of laying across scrum with loose arm could bring him into conflict with Australian referees.

CUNLIFFE JACK (Wigan)   Full back and Utility back
Age 30   Height 5ft. 8ins.   Weight 11st. 9lbs.
Upholsterer. Fine utility player able to fill any position from full back to stand-off. Toured with 1950 side, playing in final Test in Sydney as stand-off.

CAHILL TED (Rochdale)   Full back
Age 27   Height 5ft. 9ins.   Weight 12 st.
Truck-driver. Rochdale Hornets bought Cahill as full back five seasons ago. Has been five times capped for Lancashire and played so impressively for England against France and Other Nationalities. Very good defender.

O'GRADY Terry (Oldham)   Left winger
Age 19   Height 5ft. 10ins.   Weight 12st. 10lbs.
Apprentice fitter. Youngster, still growing, who was signed by Oldham when he was 16. Played for England against Wales in 1952 when 17 and had little except speed. Has shown steady improvement with experience.

JACKSON PHILIP (Barrow)   Centre
Age 22   Height 5ft. 11ins.   Weight13st. 10lbs.
Born Montreal, Canada now doing National Service in the Army. Played rugby union as stand-off and then centre. Signed by Barrow in 1950 and has played as centre with club since. Great admirer of Willie Horne, he

attributes his own sharp improvements in play in the past year to Horne's coaching.

JONES LEWIS (Leeds)   Centre
Age 23   Height 5ft. 10 ins.   Weight 12st. 6lbs.
Clerk. Lewis made his first visit to Australia in 1950 when serving in the Royal Navy. Was flown to New Zealand to take over as full back for the Great Britain Rugby Union side, then depleted by injuries. Capped for Wales at Rugby Union as full back centre and wing. Was signed by Leeds in 1953 for a fee of £6,000 sterling. After breaking arm lost confidence but just before Christmas suddenly dropped into his best form.

PRESCOTT ALAN (St. Helens)   Prop forward
Age 26   Height 5ft.11ins.   Weight 14st. 10lbs.
Storekeeper. Redheaded hard working, surprisingly fast front rower who has taken Ken Gee's place as open side prop in Test team. Played all three Tests against 1952 Australian side. Was winger with Halifax but moved to St. Helens in 1948 as loose forward. With increasing weight he moved into the front row.

ASHCROFT ERNIE (Wigan)   Centre
Age 28   Height 6ft.   Weight 13st.
Engineer. Captained Wigan this season and captained Whites in first tour trial. Toured in 1950 playing in all three Tests but didn't play in 1952 Tests against

Kangaroos. Only appearance against them was for Lancashire when he scored a try. Ankle injury at end of 1951-52 season handicapped him until 1953. Now back to best form.

GREENALL DOUG (St. Helens)   Centre
Age 26   Height 5ft. 9ins.   Weight 11st. 6lbs.
Fitter. Signed as professional when 17. Surprise selection in 1951 as right centre against touring New Zealanders in first Test. Scored a try and held his place in other two Tests. Passed over for the first Test against 1952 Kangaroos, he played in second and third. Wiry and strong, Greenall tackles very hard and has a reputation for 'fierce' exchanges, often with much heavier opponents.

BOWDEN JIM (Huddersfield)   Prop forward
Age 22   Height 6ft. 1in.   Weight 14st. 5lbs.
Played for England this season as blind side prop. Son of Herbert Bowden the Bramley hooker. Made his first-grade debut with Huddersfield in 1949 and won his Yorkshire Cap as centre in the following season. As he put on weight Bowden dropped out reappearing with Huddersfield's A team as loose forward and second rower.

TRAILL KEN (Bradford)   Loose forward
Age 27   Height 6ft.   Weight 14st.
Toured Australia and New Zealand with 1950 side, playing against New Zealand in Test. Loose forward in all three Tests against 1952 Kangaroos, where his understanding with clubmates Ernest Ward and Willie Horne and his raking kicks for touch played an important part in the home side's tactics. Played for England against Wales and Other Nationalities this season.

VALENTINE DAVID (Huddersfield)
Loose forward or second row
Age 27   Height 6ft. 1in.   Weight 13st. 10lbs.
Joiner- but now earning more money as a wrestler. Signed by Huddersfield Rugby League in 1947 and in the following season played in three Tests against 1948 Kangaroos. Injured back in 1949 and hadn't regained form when 1950 touring side was chosen.

CASTLE FRANK (Barrow)   Left winger
Age 29   Height 5ft 9ins.   Weight 12st. 6lbs.
Engineering fitter. England's fastest winger, quick to seize an opening, but somewhat doubtful under pressure and defence suspect against heavier opponents. Played in all three Tests in 1952 but left the field after 20 minutes of the final match at Bradford.

SILCOCK NAT (Wigan)   Second row.
Age 24   Height 6ft. 1in.   Weight 15st. 2lbs.
Miner. Son of famous father, also called Nat who toured
in 1932 and 1936 to Australia and won 10 'Test' Caps.
Like father, Nat is a powerful mobile forward.

PRICE RAY (Warrington)   Stand-off
Age 29   Height 5ft 7ins.   Weight 11st. 11lbs.
Changed from Rugby Union in 1947, with Belle Vue.
Transferred this season to Warrington were his pace and
foot work have made a difference to the club's attacking
play.

BOSTON WILLIAM (Wigan)   Wingman
Age 20   Height 6ft.   Weight 13st. 9lbs.
At present serving in Army at Catterick and star member
of the unit team that won Army Rugby Cup this season.
Played only a handful of games for his club since joining
them.

BURNELL ALF (Hunslet)   Scrum half
Age26   Height 5ft. 7ins.   Weight 12st. 4lbs.
Warehouseman. Played in Tests against New Zealand as
partner to Dickie Williams, who is now his team mate.
Sturdy type who has a strong hand off and a quick safe
tackle.

HELME GERRY (Warrington)   Scrum half
Age 31   Height 5ft. 6ins.   Weight 11st.
Fitter. Joined Warrington in 1945. Played against 1948
Kangaroos in all three Tests and was though to have
faded out of the picture. Made a strong come back this
season.

TURNBULL ANDREW (Leeds)   Right winger
Age 23   Height 5ft 9ins.   Weight 11st. 7lbs.
Clerk. Born in Scotland. Leeds paid £2,000 for him in
1948. Played for Britain in third Test against New
Zealand in 1951 and chosen for first Test against
Kangaroos in 1952 but had to withdraw through injury.

GUNNEY GEOFF (Hunslet)   Second row
Age 20   Height 6ft.1in.   Weight 14st. 10lbs.
Plumber. Born in Hunslet district and has come up
through three junior grades and the Hunslet second team
in five years. Has big feet (size 12 boots) and big hands.

HEDERSON JOHN (Workington)   Prop forward
Age 24   Height 5ft. 10ins.   Weight 14st. 7lbs.
Painter and decorator. Graduated from a junior club in
the Maryport district for Workington Town Club in
1949. Has played for Cumberland and for England
against Wales this season.

RAWSON HECTOR Manager
Mr Rawson has been connected with the Hunslet club for many years and is to look after financial matters on the present tour. A very knowledgeable rugby league man who will prove a capable 'treasurer' for the tourists.

HESKETH TOM Manager
Mr Hesketh from the Wigan club will take charge of team matter during the tour. He also is very knowledgeable in the sport and is looking forward to seeing Australia play on home soil.

Appearances on Tour by Players

Players	Aus	NZ	Tests Aus	Tests NZ	Tries	Goals	Pts
Cahill	8	0	0	0	0	14	28
Cunliffe	10	5	1	0	7	29	79
Boston	12	6	2	3	36	0	108
Turnbull	2	0	0	0	2	0	6
Greenall	14	7	0	1	13	0	39
Jackson	12	6	3	3	7	0	21
Ashcroft	11	4	3	2	11	0	33
Jones	13	8	3	3	8	127	278
Castle	4	1	1	0	6	0	18
O'Grady	10	7	2	3	28	0	84
Price	12	5	1	2	9	0	27
Williams	11	4	2	1	8	0	24
Burnell	10	7	0	1	9	0	27
Helme	12	4	3	2	5	0	15
Henderson	10	1	0	0	1	0	3
Prescott	13	7	3	3	1	0	3
Harris	8	6	0	2	3	0	9
McKinney	16	6	3	1	2	0	6
Bowden	13	7	2	1	2	0	6
Wilkinson	13	5	1	2	6	0	18
Briggs	11	6	0	1	4	0	12
Gunney	11	7	0	3	6	0	18
Pawsey	12	3	2	2	4	0	12
Silcock	14	5	3	0	7	0	21
Traill	11	7	1	1	1	0	3
Valentine	13	6	3	2	7	0	21

TOUR RESULTS

Date	Venue	Opponents	**Result**
May 18	Bathurst	Western Div.	W 29-11
May 22	Newcastle	Newcastle	L10-11
May 26	Wagga	Riverina	W 36-26
May 29	Sydney	Sydney	L 25-32
June 2	Wollongong	Southern Dis.	D 17-17
June 6	Sydney	NSW	L 11-22
June 12	Sydney	Australia	L 12-37
June 14	Brisbane	Brisbane	W 34-4
June 19	Brisbane	Queensland	W 34-32
June 20	Maryborough	Wide Bay	W 60-14
June 22	MacKay	Southern Zone	W 28-7
June 24	Cairns	Northern Zone	W 3918
June 27	Townsville	N. Queensland	W 39-13
June 29	Rockhampton	Cen. Queensland	W 21-12
July 3	Brisbane	Australia	W38-21
July 4	Toowoomba	Toowoomba	W 25-14
July 7	Grafton	Northern NSW	W 44-14
July 10	Sydney	NSW	L6-17***
July 17	Sydney	Australia	L 16-20
July 21	Whangarei	Auckland Maori	W 14-4
July 24	Auckland	New Zealand	W 27-7
July 27	Wellington	Wellington	W 61-18
July 31	Greymouth	New Zealand	L 14-20
Aug. 4	Dunedin	South Island	W 32-11

Aug. 7	Christchurch	Canterbury	W 60-14
Aug. 9	New Plymouth	North Island	W 42-7
Aug. 11	Hamilton	South Auckland	W 26-14
Aug.14	Auckland	New Zealand	W 12-6
Aug. 16.	Auckland	Auckland	L 4-5
Aug.18	Sydney	NSW	L 15-35
Aug. 21	Canberra	Southern Dist	W 66-21
Aug. 23	Maitland	Newcastle	L 22-28

APPENDIX ONE

Australia and New Zealand in the USA

With the first ever World Cup competition in France completed both Australia and New Zealand travelled home via the USA in order to play two exhibition games in California. The two games would be the first ever professional rugby league games to be played in the United States. I suppose that both the Antipodean authorities along with the home counterparts were hoping that it would lead to a foothold being established for the game in California.

The council decided that the two games needed to be handled by a top referee so to that end they assigned Ron Gelder to travel across the Atlantic with both sets of players. Gelder was accompanied by the then Secretary of the Rugby League Bill Fallowfield who was to assess the whole affair and report back to council. Also, the eminent official Harry Sutherland was dispatched to acquaint the Californian press with the correct terminology for the new game. The whole project was the brain child of an American with an interest in the game.

The teams had an eventful crossing of the Atlantic which took over twenty-two hours. Unlike today the aircraft made the journey in short hops, from London to Reykjavik in Iceland. From there they flew to Gander in

Canada before the flight down to New York. It was the same story on the trip out to Los Angeles with that journey taking twelve hours.

While all efforts were made the start was the most inauspicious it could have been when the first game was scheduled to get under way on Friday 26th November. The game to be played at Veterans Memorial Stadium Lasted all of five minutes!

When the game kicked off it was the Australians who went onto the attack and crossed for the first try. The honour of scoring the first points in the USA fell to Ken Kearney and Pidding added the extra two. The game was very soon called off as fog quickly blanketed the field. So thick was the fog that referee Gelder told reporters **"The bloomin' fog is worse than London's."** When the game had kicked off the officials had difficulty seeing the players but once the first try had been scored it became impossible for the referee and touch judges to see a hand in front of their face. They called the game off and the crowd of around a thousand were informed that the game would be re-scheduled for the following day, the Saturday at the same venue.

The local newspaper The Independent Press-Telegraph covered the game and the report is reproduced below.

Photograph courtesy of Terry Williams at the NRL Museum

"A powerful Australian team fought its way to a 30-13 triumph over New Zealand Saturday before approx. 1000 fans at Veterans Memorial Stadium in the first professional rugby game ever played in the Unites States. The win was a second in a row for Australia and clinched its first victory in five series with the Kiwis four previous series netting them two wins and two ties for New Zealand.

The Kangaroos demonstrated far superior passing ability, spotted the Kiwis three points in the opening seconds of play, took the lead in the eight minutes later and never relinquished it.

Although new to most of the rabid fans action in the second half and the underdog Kiwis even had a loosely organised rooting section throughout the final period.

Famed British commentator Harry Sunderland explained at half time that, "Rugby is hard but not rough: rugged but not dirty." If the second half of play was not "rough' and "dirty" then the Rams, Cardinals and 49ers have been playing drop the handkerchief this year.

The entire second half was marked by bone-jarring, paddingless tackles, flying elbows, knees and feet, which had the fans moaning in sympathy. Two New Zealand players goal kicker Scotty McKay and

Neville Denton were injured and had to leave the field but returned into the midst of the organised 'mayhem' after several minutes 'recuperative leave.'

New Zealand opened the scoring with the game only 30 seconds old when Denton cut through intercepted a pass and ran 35 yards for a try (touchdown) MacKay's try for goal (conversion kick) was wide and the Kiwis led 3-0.

However, Harry Wells 198 pound Australian speedster scored from 10 yards out eight minutes later and Noel Pidding kicked the goal to give the Kangaroos a 5-3 lead.

Australia took a 10-3 margin into the half time intermission when forward (lineman) Brian Davies scored on a 50 yard play down the sidelines. Pidding kicked the goal from a difficult angle his second of six successful two-pointers.

The second half scoring opened as Norm Provan scored on a short run to give Australia a 15-3 lead and from that point the Kangaroos had the game in their pouch.

A spectacular run by Davies who raced to within five yards of the goal and then passed to Ken Kearney gave the Aussies a 20-3 margin.

Captain Cyril Eastlake 163 pound New Zealand star who was a stand out for the Kiwis all day, cut that margin with the finest run of the game midway in the second half. He bowled over two would be tacklers, carried to within four yards of the goal then lateralled to John Yates. Yates a mammoth Maori native dove into scoring territory for three points. Once again MacKay missed a tough angled kick at goal and Australia led 20-6.

The Kangaroos added five additional points on a Davies 10 yard smash and another difficult kick by Pidding to roll into a 25-6 lead before Eastlake made good on a penalty kick, ran back an interception for a successful try and kicked goal to cut the margin to 25-13.

The final try came on another long run back of an interception by Australian Wells.

The two teams renew their battling in a rematch today at 2.45pm. at the Los Angeles Coliseum."

It is interesting to note the way in which the game was portrayed by the local American reporters used to covering both American and Canadian football. The other point worth noting is just how rough and dirty they considered the game to be when comparing it to their own brand of football. The attendance of around 1000 was not as high as expected and perhaps contributed to the decision of both combatants as well as the British in not following up on the enterprise. We have no way of knowing how many turned up on the Friday evening fogbound game.

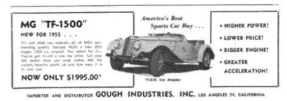

Souvenir Program   Price
                                                        25¢

AUSTRALIAN *Kangaroos*
VS.
NEW ZEALAND *Kiwis*
Rugby League Football — 2:45 P.M.
★ ★ ★
LATIN ALL STARS
VS.
AMERICAN ALL STARS
Soccer Football — 12:30 P.M.
★ ★ ★
LOS ANGELES MEMORIAL COLISEUM
Sunday, November 28, 1954

MG "TF-1500"   America's Best
NEW FOR 1955 . . .   Sports Car Buy . . .   • HIGHER POWER!
                                                    • LOWER PRICE!
                                                    • BIGGER ENGINE!
                                                    • GREATER
NOW ONLY $1995.00°   ACCELERATION!

IMPORTER AND DISTRIBUTOR GOUGH INDUSTRIES, INC. LOS ANGELES 34, CALIFORNIA

Photograph courtesy of Terry Williams at the NRL Museum.

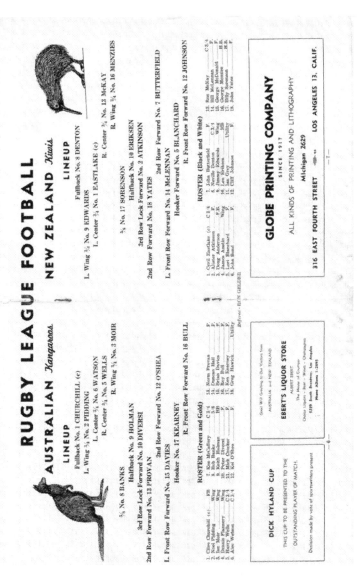

RUGBY LEAGUE FOOTBALL

AUSTRALIAN Kangaroos

LINEUP

Fullback No. 1 CHURCHILL (c)
L. Wing ¾ No. 2 PIDDING
L. Center ¾ No. 6 WATSON
R. Center ¾ No. 5 WELLS
R. Wing ¾ No. 3 MOIR
¾ No. 8 BANKS
Halfback No. 9 HOLMAN
3rd Row Lock Forward No. 10 DIVERSI
2nd Row Forward No. 13 PROVAN
2nd Row Forward No. 15 DAVIES
Hooker No. 17 KEARNEY
L. Front Row Forward No. 12 OSHEA
R. Front Row Forward No. 16 BULL

ROSTER (Green and Gold)

1. Clive Churchill (c) ... FB
2. Noel Pidding ... Wing
3. ... Wing
4. Dennis Flannery ... Wing
5. Harry Wells ... C¾
6. Alex Watson ...
7. Ken McCaffery ... C¾
8. Rob Banks ... ¾
9. Keith Holman ... H.B.
10. Peter Diversi ... F
31. Mick Crocker ... F
12. Sid O'Shea ... F
13. Norm Provan ... F
14. Duncan Hall ... F
15. Brian Davies ... F
16. Rory Bull ... F
17. Ken Kearney ... F
18. Greg Hawick ... UMPRY

NEW ZEALAND Kiwis

LINEUP

Fullback No. 8 DENTON
L. Wing ¾ No. 9 EDWARDS
L. Center ¾ No. 1 EASTLAKE (c)
R. Center ¾ No. 13 McKAY
R. Wing ¾ No. 16 MENZIES
¾ No. 17 SORENSON
Halfback No. 10 ERIKSEN
3rd Row Lock Forward No. 2 ATKINSON
2nd Row Forward No. 18 YATES
2nd Row Forward No. 7 BUTTERFIELD
Hooker Forward No. 14 McLENNAN
L. Front Row Forward No. 5 BLANCHARD
R. Front Row Forward No. 12 JOHNSON

ROSTER (Black and White)

1. Cyril Eastlake (c) ... C¾
2. Alister Atkinson ... F
3. Jimmy Edwards ... F.B.
4. James Austin ... Wing
5. Lori Blanchard ... F
6. John Bond ... F
7. John Butterfield ... F
8. Neville Denton ... C¾
9. Tommy Edwards ... Wing
10. Les Eriksen ... HB
11. Ian Grey ... Utility
12. Cliff Johnson ... F
13. Ron McKay ... C¾
14. Bill McLennan ... F
15. George McDonald ... F.B.
16. George Menzies ... R.B.
17. Billy Sorensen ... H.B.
18. John Yates ... F

GLOBE PRINTING COMPANY

SINCE 1917

ALL KINDS OF PRINTING AND LITHOGRAPHY

Michigan 2629

316 EAST FOURTH STREET   LOS ANGELES 13, CALIF.

DICK HYLAND CUP

THIS CUP TO BE PRESENTED TO THE OUTSTANDING PLAYER OF MATCH.

Decision made by vote of sportswriters present

EBERT'S LIQUOR STORE

ALBERT EBERT

The House of Courtesy

Choice Liquors - Beer - Wines - Champagnes

5299 South Broadway, Los Angeles
Phone Adams 1-2895

Good Will Greeting to Our Visitors from AUSTRALIA and NEW ZEALAND

Photograph courtesy of Terry Williams at the NRL Museum.

The second game which was played at the Olympic Stadium, The Coliseum in Los Angeles attracted very little coverage in the local newspaper. I suppose that was to be expected as it followed so quickly the first encounter and it was the second such game. Even the Press Association coverage sent over to Australia and New Zealand was very brief simply giving the score and scorers in most cases. In the vast stadium the crowd of 4554 would have been lost and certainly would have produce little atmosphere.

With the games over all returned home and the game settled back into its own cosy parochial existence and nothing further was really attempted to establish the game in the United States.

Printed in Great Britain
by Amazon

51200458R00104